P9-BYX-451

Still a Man's World

MEN AND MASCULINITY

Michael Kimmel, editor

Still a Man's World

Men Who Do "Women's Work"

Christine L. Williams

UNIVERSITY OF CALIFORNIA PRESS
BERKELEY LOS ANGELES LONDON

University of California Press
Berkeley and Los Angeles, California

University of California Press, Ltd.
London, England
© 1995 by
The Regents of the University of California

Library of Congress Cataloging-in-Publication Data

Williams, Christine L., 1959–
    Still a man's world : men who do "women's work" / Christine L.
Williams.
        p.   cm. — (Men and masculinity)
    Includes bibliographical references and index.
    ISBN 0-520-08787-9 (pbk. : alk. paper)
    1. Sex role in the work environment.   2. Sex discrimination
against men.   3. Sex discrimination in employment.   4. Stereotype
(Psychology)   I. Title.   II. Series: Men and masculinity (Berkeley,
Calif.)
    HD6060.6.W55   1995
    306.3'615—dc20   94-29009
                                                                              CIP

Printed in the United States of America

08 07 06 05 04
9 8 7 6 5 4 3

The paper used in this publication meets the minimum requirements of
ANSI/NISO Z39.48-1992 (R 1997) (*Permanence of Paper*). ∞

Contents

Tables

Acknowledgments

I am very grateful to many people who contributed to this project. I owe the greatest debt to the men and women I interviewed, whose candor and generosity made this book possible. In addition, I would like to give special thanks to Martin Button and Mary Waters, for reading and commenting on several drafts of this manuscript; Michael Kimmel, for enthusiastically supporting this project from its inception; and Deb Umberson and Bob and Mary Jo Nye, for their last-minute advice and encouragement. I am also grateful to Naomi Schneider, my editor, for shepherding this manuscript through the University of California Press and to Will Murphy, Rose Anne White, and Steve Gilmartin for their production assistance. And I thank my friends, colleagues, and graduate students at the University of Texas for their helpful suggestions and encouragement, especially Lynne Attwood, David Austin, Dana Britton, Margaret Johnson, Dale MacLemore, and Terry Sullivan.

In addition to those who gave me intellectual support, I am indebted to many people who provided me with "structural" support. My deepest thanks to Ken and Margaret Bock, Mary Waters, and Mom and Dad for putting me up (and putting up with me) while I was conducting this research. The Sociology Departments of Arizona State University, the University of California at Berkeley, and Harvard University gave me offices, phones, and visiting scholar status, which greatly facilitated my research. This project was funded in part by the University Research Institute at the University of Texas at Austin.

For their assistance in contacting respondents, I would like to thank (in Texas) Debra Hughes, Pat MacLemore, David Austin, Roy Dalrymple, Greta Gilbertson, Brendan Kenny, Jimmy Burnett, Mary Cris Crawford, and Julie Brandt; (in California) David Levin, Terry Strathman, Jean Margolis, Elsa Trantor, Nancy Tennebaum, and Laurie Wermuth; (in Massachusetts) Mary Waters, Ann Hornsby, Cheri Minton, Victoria Kent, Margaret Waters, Borgie Bruner, and Nicholas Nova; (in Arizona) Bernard Farber, Esther Hardesty, Rose Weitz, Ronnelle Paulsen, and Julie August. Thanks also to Ricardo Gonzalez for his creative title recommendations (my favorite being, "My collar may be pink, but it still has a ring around it").

I dedicate this book to my mother and father, Bunnie and Clyde Williams, for their love and patience (and my original inspiration to study gender segregation); to my sisters, Cathie and Karrie, and their families, for their friendship and support over the years (and their valiant efforts to stay awake during my television debut); to my fellow travelers, Mary and Deb, for their confidence and solidarity throughout the writing, revising, and tenuring process; and to Martin, for everything.

1

Gendered Jobs and Gendered Workers

A 1959 article in *Library Journal* entitled "The Male Librarian—An Anomaly?" begins this way:

> My friends keep trying to get me out of the library.
> ... Library work is fine, they agree, but they smile
> and shake their heads benevolently and charitably,
> as if it were unnecessary to add that it is one of the
> dullest, most poorly paid, unrewarding, off-beat ac-
> tivities any man could be consigned to. If you have
> a heart condition, if you're physically handicapped
> in other ways, well, such a job is a blessing. And for
> women there's no question library work is fine; there
> are some wonderful women in libraries and we all
> ought to be thankful to them. But let's face it, no
> healthy man of normal intelligence should go into
> it.[1]

Male librarians still face this treatment today, as do other
men who work in predominantly female occupations. In
1990, my local newspaper featured a story entitled "Men
Still Avoiding Women's Work" that described my research

on men in nursing, librarianship, teaching, and social work. Soon afterwards, a humor columnist for the same paper wrote a spoof on the story that he titled, "Most Men Avoid Women's Work because It Is Usually So Boring."[2] The columnist poked fun at hairdressing, librarianship, nursing, and babysitting—in his view, all "lousy" jobs requiring low intelligence and a high tolerance for boredom. Evidently people still wonder why any "healthy man of normal intelligence" would willingly work in a "woman's occupation."

In fact, not very many men do work in these fields, although their numbers are growing. In 1990, over 500,000 men were employed in these four occupations, constituting approximately 6 percent of all registered nurses, 15 percent of all elementary school teachers, 17 percent of all librarians, and 32 percent of all social workers. These percentages have fluctuated in recent years: As table 1 indicates, librarianship and social work have undergone slight declines in the proportions of men since 1975; teaching has remained somewhat stable; while nursing has experienced noticeable gains. The number of men in nursing actually doubled between 1980 and 1990; however, their overall proportional representation remains very low.

Very little is known about these men who "cross over" into these nontraditional occupations. While numerous books have been written about women entering male-dominated occupations, few have asked why men are underrepresented in traditionally female jobs.[3] The underlying assumption in most research on gender and work is that, given a free choice, both men and women would work in predominantly male occupations, as they are generally better paying and more prestigious than predominantly female occupations. The few men who will-

Table 1
*Men in the "Women's Professions":
Number (in thousands) and Distribution of Men
Employed in the Occupations, Selected Years*

Profession	1975	1980	1990
Registered Nurses			
Number of men	28	46	92
% men	3.0	3.5	5.5
Elementary Teachers[a]			
Number of men	194	225	223
% men	14.6	16.3	14.8
Librarians			
Number of men	34	27	32
% men	18.9	14.8	16.7
Social Workers			
Number of men	116	134	179
% men	39.2	35.0	31.8

SOURCES: U.S. Department of Labor, Bureau of Labor Statistics, *Employment and Earnings* 38, no. 1 (January 1991), table 22 (employed civilians by detailed occupation), p. 185; vol. 28, no. 1 (January 1981), table 23 (employed persons by detailed occupation), p. 180; vol. 22, no. 7 (January 1976), table 2 (employed persons by detailed occupation), p. 11.
[a]Excludes kindergarten teachers.

ingly "cross over" must be, as the 1959 article suggests, "anomalies."

Popular culture reinforces the belief that these men are "anomalies." Men are rarely portrayed working in these occupations, and when they are, they are represented in extremely stereotypical ways. For example, in the 1990 movie *Kindergarten Cop*, muscle-man Arnold Schwarzenegger played a detective forced to work undercover as a kindergarten teacher; the otherwise competent Schwarzenegger was completely overwhelmed by the five-year-old children in his class. A television series in the early

1990s about a male elementary school teacher (*Drexell's Class*) stars a lead character who *hates children*. The implication of these popular shows is that any "real man" would have nothing to do with this kind of job; indeed, a "real man" would be incapable of working in a "woman's profession."

This book challenges these stereotypes about men who do "women's work" through case studies of men in four predominantly female occupations: nursing, elementary school teaching, librarianship, and social work. I show that men maintain their masculinity in these occupations, despite the popular stereotypes. Moreover, male power and privilege is preserved and reproduced in these occupations through a complex interplay between gendered expectations embedded in organizations, and the gendered interests workers bring with them to their jobs. Each of these occupations is "still a man's world" even though mostly women work in them.

I selected these four professions as case studies of men who do "women's work" for a variety of reasons. First, because they are so strongly associated with women and femininity in our popular culture, these professions highlight and perhaps even exaggerate the barriers and advantages men face when entering predominantly female environments. Second, they each require extended periods of educational training and apprenticeship, requiring individuals in these occupations to be at least somewhat committed to their work (unlike those employed in, say, clerical or domestic work). Therefore I thought they would be reflective about their decisions to join these "nontraditional" occupations, making them "acute observers" and, hence, ideal informants about the sort of social and psychological processes I am interested in de-scribing.⁴ Third, these occupations vary a great deal in the proportion of men working in them. Although my aim was not to engage in between-group comparisons, I be-lieved that the proportions of men in a work setting would strongly influence the degree to which they felt ac-cepted and satisfied with their jobs.⁵

I traveled across the United States conducting in-depth interviews with seventy-six men and twenty-three women who work in nursing, teaching, librarianship, and social work. Like the people employed in these professions gen-erally, those in my sample were predominantly white (90 percent). Their ages ranged from twenty to sixty-six, and the average age was thirty-eight. I interviewed women as well as men to gauge their feelings and reactions to men's entry into "their" professions. Respondents were inten-tionally selected to represent a wide range of specialties and levels of education and experience. I interviewed stu-dents in professional schools, "front line" practitioners, administrators, and retirees, asking them about their mo-tivations to enter these professions, their on-the-job ex-periences, and their opinions about men's status and prospects in these fields.⁶

The link between masculinity and work has only re-cently become a topic for sociological investigation. Al-though many books have been written about male work-ers, most contain no analysis of gender. They may tell us a great deal about the meanings, purposes, and aspira-tions that characterize men's working lives, but not how masculinity relates to these general concerns. On the other hand, most of the research that does address gender and work has focused on women and on their struggles to achieve economic equality with men. Women currently constitute 45 percent of the paid labor force, but they continue to lag behind men in earnings and organizational power.[7] Several books and articles now document this economic disparity and explain it in terms of the different meanings, purposes, and aspirations that women *qua women* experience in the labor force. In other words, in the sociology of work, gender seems to be something that affects only women, and affects them only negatively.

To explain how and why a woman's gender impedes her economic success, two general theoretical approaches have been developed. On the one hand, conventional theories—such as human capital or status attainment theory—attribute women's lesser achievement in the workplace to the gender characteristics that women bring with them to work. According to this perspective, women cannot compete as successfully as men for the best jobs either because they were not properly socialized to acquire highly valued worker characteristics (such as aggressiveness and ambition), or because they have competing household responsibilities. If men are more successful, this argument goes, that is because they have superior skills or they have made better organizational choices.[8]

Feminist researchers have generally rejected this perspective, claiming instead that women's lesser achievement is due to gender discrimination and sexual harassment, not to women's supposed deficiencies compared to men.[9] In fact, several studies have demonstrated that women and men are not treated equally at work, even if they possess the same qualifications and are hired to perform the same job. In nearly every occupation, women encounter barriers when they try to enter the most lucrative and prestigious specialties. A "glass ceiling" prevents them from reaching the top positions.[10] From this perspective, the organizational dynamics—and not the "feminine" attributes of women—result in women's lesser pay and status in the work world.

One of the most important studies documenting this organizational inequality is Rosabeth Moss Kanter's *Men and Women of the Corporation*. In this book, Kanter argues that the barriers women face in predominantly male occupations can be attributed to their *numerical* minority in organizations. Although men and women may have similar qualifications, the organizational structure nevertheless promotes gender differentiation through the mechanism of tokenism. She maintains that because all tokens "stand out" from the dominant group and receive more than their fair share of attention, they are therefore subjected to stereotyping, role entrapment, and various other forms of marginalization.

Kanter based her theory of tokenism on a study of women in a major U.S. corporation, but she argued that the harassment and discrimination women encountered there would affect a member of *any* token minority group. This is a problematic assumption, but her exclusive focus on women precluded a systematic analysis of this claim. However, Kanter did provide two individual examples of tokens who were male to illustrate her point; rather fortuitously, one of these was the case of a male nurse:

> One male nursing student whom I interviewed reported that he thought he would enjoy being the only man in a group of women. Then he found that he engendered a great deal of hostility and that he was teased every time he failed to live up to a manly image—e.g., if he was vague or subjective in speech.

The *content* of interaction when men are tokens may appear to give them an elevated position, but the process is still one of role encapsulation and treating tokens as symbols. Deference can be a patronizing reminder of difference, too.[11]

Token dynamics clearly do affect the men who do "women's work." Like Kanter, I found that when men enter nursing and other predominantly female professions, they are treated differently from women: They tend to receive preferential consideration in hiring; they are channeled into certain male-identified specialties; and they are pressured to perform specific job tasks that are identified as "manly." But unlike women tokens, men apparently *benefit* from this special treatment: As Kanter herself points out, men are "elevated" by their token status. They make more money than women (on average) in each of these occupations, and they are greatly overrepresented in administrative positions. The theory of tokenism, developed to explain discrimination against women in nontraditional occupations, ironically does not account for the very different consequences of minority status for men and women.

Kanter's study is a good example of how the exclusive focus on women in the research on gender and work has resulted in an incomplete theoretical picture of how the work world discriminates against women. To fully understand the source of women's disadvantages in the workplace, it is essential to examine the source of men's advantages. Shifting the focus to men therefore is not intended to abandon the concerns of women, but rather to implicate men in the overall pattern of discrimination against women. However, including men's experiences in the analysis of gender and work does substantially alter the research questions: Instead of asking, "What are the deficiencies of women?" or "What are the barriers to women?" the questions now become, "Why is gender a liability for women but an asset for men?" and "What are the mechanisms that propel men to more successful careers?"

To address these questions, I rely on a theory of "gendered organizations."[12] According to this perspective, cultural beliefs about masculinity and femininity are built into the very structure of the work world. Organizational hierarchies, job descriptions, and informal workplace practices all contain deeply embedded assumptions about the gender and gendered characteristics of workers. These beliefs about gender—which are often unstated and unacknowledged—limit women's opportunities while enhancing men's occupational success. In other words, work organizations contain built-in advantages for men that are often unnoticed; indeed, they seem like natural or inevitable characteristics of all organizations.

On the most basic level, work organizations are gendered in that employers prefer to hire workers with few if any nonwork distractions. This is not a gender-neutral preference: Men fit this description far more easily than women, because of the unequal division of household labor in most families. Joan Acker writes,

> The closest the disembodied worker doing the abstract job comes to a real worker is the male worker whose life centers on his full-time, life-long job, while his wife or another woman takes care of his personal needs and his children.[13]

Women's careers often suffer because work organizations typically do not accommodate their additional household responsibilities.[14]

This organizational preference for men exists even in

the "women's professions." An Arizona nursing director who is in charge of hiring the staff of the emergency room explained why men in his hospital are overrepresented in the best positions:

> I've sometimes stopped to wonder whether there is a little bias there. I'm not sure. . . . The men sometimes tend to be a little more stable than the women. A lot of the men who work in the ER [emergency room] have really been here for quite a while. They're married; most have kids. When it's time to have a baby, they're not the ones who take off. It's the same problem, it's really not a lot different than a lot of other professions.

Although organizations that employ nurses and members of the other "women's professions" often permit leaves-of-absence to tend to family responsibilities, no one is actually rewarded for taking this time off. Instead, those who demonstrate unconditional devotion to their work receive the best jobs, giving men an unfair advantage over women even in these "female" occupations.

There is a second, even more profound way that organizations are deeply gendered, and that is through the hierarchical division of labor. Gender segregation exists in nearly every organization and every occupation, with men occupying the best paying and most prestigious jobs, and the highest positions of organizational power.[15] In the United States, more than half of all men or women would have to change major job categories to equalize the proportions of men and women in all occupations. This overall degree of segregation has changed remarkably little over the past hundred years, despite radical transformations in the U.S. job market.[16] Technological developments and management directives have created millions of new jobs and eliminated others, but the basic structure of the gendered division of labor has remained intact. Largely because of this division of labor, women earn far less than men: On average, women still receive less than seventy-five cents for every dollar earned by a man.[17]

According to the theory of gendered organizations, the division of labor by gender favors men because organizations value men and qualities associated with masculinity more highly than they value women. Organizational hierarchies reify the male standard, rewarding only those who possess putatively masculine characteristics with promotion to the best positions. This preference for masculinity seems to happen regardless of the proportional representation of men in an occupation.

In fact, the higher value placed on men and masculinity is especially evident in traditionally female professions, where men are the tokens. Men have been overrepresented in the top positions in these occupations ever since the nineteenth century, when women were first actively recruited into them. At that time, employers deliberately set aside jobs in administration and management for men because they believed that these positions required the job holder to be level-headed, impartial, technically proficient, and even aggressive.[18] All of these qualities were associated with white, middle-class masculinity. Black men and newly arriving immigrant men typically were not believed to possess these highly touted traits; they were definitely not among those recruited for the top positions. The middle-class white men who did enter these jobs were rewarded for their "masculine" qualities with higher salaries than women received. Also, men were paid more because employers assumed that unlike women, these men needed extra money to support a dependent spouse and children.

Men still are overrepresented in the most prestigious and best-paying specialties in these occupations. Today, male nurses tend to specialize in certain "high tech" areas (such as intensive care and emergency room nursing) or in areas that demand a high degree of physical strength (such as psychiatric and orthopedic nursing), and they are overrepresented in administration. Men in elementary school teaching typically teach the upper grades (fourth through sixth), and they often supplement their teaching with coaching or administrative work. Male librarians concentrate in the high technology computer information specialties and administration, and they are more likely than female librarians to work in major academic and public libraries. And male social workers tend to work in corrections and in administration. Men are drawn to specialties associated with stereotypical masculine qualities, such as strength, technical proficiency and managerial ability. Indeed, in some organizations, these specialties have become all-male enclaves.

Many men entering these professions today anticipate working in these masculine enclaves. But others find themselves pressured into these specialties despite their inclinations otherwise. That is, some men who prefer to work in the more "feminine" specialties—such as pediatric nursing or children's librarianship—encounter inexorable pressures to "move up," a phenomenon I refer to as the "glass escalator effect." Like being on an invisible "up" escalator, men must struggle to remain in the lower (i.e., "feminine") levels of their professions.

Some organizations mandate this gender segregation through policies that prevent men from working in the most female-identified specialties. For example, some hospitals bar male nurses from working in obstetrics and gynecology wards, and some school districts prohibit the hiring of men as kindergarten teachers.[19] These prohibitions are motivated in part by fears of men's sexuality: The assumption is that only men who are child molesters or sexual perverts would be drawn to these specialties. In these instances, gender is an overt part of the job description.

But often the pressures that move men into the more "masculine" specialties are more subtle than this, embedded in informal interactions that take place between men and their supervisors, co-workers, and clients. For instance, physicians occasionally ask male nurses their opinions on medical issues (practically unheard of among female nurses), and this can contribute to the promotion of the male nurses to supervisory positions.[20] Male supervisors sometimes share an interest in sports or other hobbies with their male employees which can lead to male bonding and camaraderie in the workplace, thereby enhancing men's chances for successful careers. Because most of the organizations that train and employ nurses, librarians, teachers, and social workers are "male-dominated," men are often in positions to make decisions that favor other men.

In addition to supervisors, women colleagues and clients often have highly gendered expectations of the men working in these professions that can contribute to men's advancement. For example, some men told me they were pushed into leadership positions by female colleagues, who believed men to be better able to represent their interests to male management. Even the negative stereotypes held by the public can sometimes escalate men into higher positions: A librarian working in the children's collection of a public library made some parents uncomfortable (according to his supervisors), so he was transferred to the adult reference division—resulting in a promotion and an increase in pay. While some men may be uncomfortable with these expectations—and some probably leave these professions because of them—those who remain and conform to them are often rewarded with the higher status and pay this special treatment can bring.

Women who work in these professions are also constrained by beliefs about gender, but for women, others' beliefs about femininity and female sexuality tend to limit instead of enhance their professional opportunities. Women who work in these professions are expected to possess such feminine attributes as care-giving, service orientation, and sexual availability and attractiveness— all qualities associated with women's traditional domestic functions. These attributes are often emphasized in popular media portrayals of women in these occupations: Female nurses, librarians, social workers, and school teachers are typically represented as pseudo-wives, mothers, or unmarried daughters of their male bosses or supervisors, and they are often sexually fetishized in these roles. The perennially popular movie *It's a Wonderful Life* contrasts Donna Reed as happily married wife and mother with an image of her as a dowdy, spinster librarian, complete with tight bun, glasses, and nervous, repressed sexuality. Card shops and video stores contain myriad examples of women nurses portrayed as sexy nymphomaniacs or castrating battle-axes. These cultural representations filter into the actual practice of these jobs: Because many of the women in these occupations work under the direct control and supervision of heterosexual men, they are often subjected to sexual flirtations, bosses' requests for nonwork favors, and outright sexual harassment.[21]

This is not to claim, however, that there is any necessary or inevitable connection between these jobs and femininity. Prior to the nineteenth century, when most teachers, nurses, and librarians were men, these occupations did not connote femininity and female sexuality as they do today. Moreover, many working in these jobs perform administrative or highly technical tasks that do not involve any so-called "feminine" qualities. Nevertheless, once gendered expectations are embedded in jobs, workers are assumed to possess the appropriate gendered attributes; they may even be evaluated on how well they conform to these expectations.[22] But because feminine qualities are devalued, by conforming to gendered expectations, a woman does not usually enhance her economic prospects within organizations. Engaging in heterosexual flirtations and affairs has been shown to be especially damaging to women's careers, even when women are willing participants.[23]

Organizations thus treat men and women very differently regardless of their proportional representation in an occupation. The workplace is not gender-neutral; it is a central site for the creation and reproduction of gender differences and gender inequality. Both men and women are constrained to act in certain ways by organizational hierarchies, job descriptions, and informal workplace practices that are based on deeply embedded assumptions about masculinity and femininity, but this social construction of gender favors men by rewarding them for the "masculine" qualities they are presumed to bring with them to the workplace.

Workers are not passive players in this social reproduction of gender in organizations. The theory of gendered organizations recognizes that workers themselves are gendered: Men and women bring different and often competing interests and desires to work, and they actively struggle to remake organizational structure to reflect these interests. But unlike human capital theory, this perspective maintains that gender attributes are not given and uniform, nor are they necessarily rational. The gendered interests brought to work by individuals are constantly being negotiated in a dialectical process with the gendered structure of organizations. As Cynthia Cockburn writes: "People have a gender, and their gender rubs off on the jobs they do. The jobs in turn have a gender character which rubs off on the people who do them."[24] When workers act on the basis of their perceived collective interests as men or women, they contribute to the "gendering" of organizations.

American labor history is full of examples of men organizing collectively in the workplace to promote and protect their perceived gender interests. For many men, their sense of themselves as masculine is closely associated with the technical skills, male bonding, and the breadwinner ethic of the workplace; success at work often constitutes *proof* of their masculinity. Working alongside women can be deeply threatening to men's sense of pride and self-esteem, so many have vigorously defended gender segregation by establishing barriers to women and treating the few who cross over with scorn and derision.[25]

In addition to asserting their masculinity, men have also used the workplace to consolidate their power over women and their privileges in society. Men have occasionally organized to resist the entry of women into "their" occupations as a means to protect their higher wages and exclusive access to the best jobs, couching their demands in terms of their duties and rights as men in society.[26]

Women have also at times used gendered discourses to defend *their* rights to work.[27] But overall, women have been much more active than men in challenging the gendered division of labor by crossing over into nontraditional occupations, and accepting the few token men who enter "their" occupations.[28] Part of the reason for this difference is that unlike men, women stand to benefit economically from crossing over. But also, occupational integration does not seem to threaten women's gender identity in the same fundamental psychological way as it threatens men's sense of themselves as masculine. While many women may enjoy the "feminine" aspects of their work, their femininity is not contingent on proving themselves competent in "gender-appropriate" work, which is often how masculinity is experienced by men.[29]

However, when men enter predominantly female professions, they do not abandon their gender identity (despite the stereotypes about them), nor do they lose their interest in sustaining male privilege in society. Some men eagerly pursue administration and other "masculine" specialties for the higher pay and status, and for the opportunity these positions offer to consolidate and affirm their gender identity. Even those who work alongside women in the same specialty often will play up their masculinity, emphasizing their difference from women. Men creatively appropriate tasks or even aspects of tasks that can be labeled "masculine" to legitimize their presence in these fields. For example, some male nurses claim they bring special insight and experience to the care of male patients, especially in performing tasks like catheterization. A male reference librarian at an urban public library believes that men are needed to control angry and potentially violent patrons. A male kindergarten teacher brings his banjo to class; another uses his class to test market the children's books that he writes. And social workers in children's protective services talk about being masculine role models for the male children. The various strategies men employ to emphasize their masculinity and distance themselves from their female colleagues help to quell concerns that they are effeminate—while adding to their prospects for further advancement in these fields.

Of course, not all men are equally committed to maintaining an image of themselves as suitably "masculine." Among those I interviewed were feminist men and gay men, some of whom chose their occupations precisely because they rejected conventional expectations about masculinity. Some racial/ethnic minority men also articulated alternative motives for participating in these occupations, such as the desire to engage in community activism. Nevertheless, those who do not conform to the socially sanctioned ideal of masculinity often are faced with considerable dilemmas: In some cases, their refusal to conform resulted in career sanctions, such as being passed over for promotion or even being fired. Gay men are particularly vulnerable to such job actions, leading some to publicly display the appropriately "masculine" characteristics while privately disavowing them.

Thus, workers are gendered, but men do not necessarily share identical gender interests. Moreover, the meaning and importance of masculinity is not fixed: It is continually reconstructed and renegotiated at work. As David Morgan writes,

> Gender does not in any straightforward way arise out of the workplace, nor is it a set of characteristics

which are brought, like lunch boxes, into the workplace by employees. Rather, there is an interaction
between employees and workplace . . . and gender
becomes one of the ways, very often one of the most
important ways through which individuals make
sense of or structure their daily environment. . . .
Men and women introduce some degree of fixity and
control over what is often a dynamic, changing, and
sometimes threatening situation. [This] is also a way
in which men exercise some degree of control, for-
mally and informally, over other men and women.[30]

There is a complex interplay between the gendered expectations embedded in organizations, and the needs and
desires brought to the workplace by individual men. This
book explores this dialectic for men in predominantly female professions.[31] Their efforts and experiences highlight, and perhaps even exaggerate the ways that gender
differences and male domination are reproduced in
organizations.

The next chapter describes how expectations about
gender became embedded in these occupations. Teaching, nursing, librarianship, and social work were first defined as "women's work" in the nineteenth century. Due
to large-scale economic and demographic changes following the U.S. Civil War, women were tapped for jobs
that previously employed only men. Cultural beliefs
about women's nature and their proper place in society
were used to justify women's employment in these areas.
Women were among those active in defining these as appropriate occupations for women.

In the twentieth century, concerns about their occupations' low status and pay prompted the leaders in nurs-

ing, teaching, librarianship, and social work to reassess the gendered assumptions about their work. The predominantly female composition of these fields was increasingly seen as a barrier to "professionalization," and concerted efforts were undertaken to recruit more men to solve this problem. The work was gradually redefined again—but this time as appropriate for career-oriented men, who, it was hoped, would flock to these beleaguered occupations and bring with them higher salaries and prestige. These strategies have achieved only limited success, but clearly they enhanced the opportunities available to the few men willing to "cross over"—and they continue to have this effect today.

The book then turns to the current status of men in these occupations. Chapter 3 discusses the reasons men enter these fields and examines the reactions of their friends and families to their decision to do "women's work." Because of the unique circumstances of their recruitment, several men in this study did not view their occupational choices as inconsistent with masculinity, nor did they see themselves as "trailblazers" into nontraditional jobs. The men in my sample are not "anomalies": In many ways they are "typical" men who for various reasons ended up doing "untypical" work.

Chapter 4 then examines their experiences in professional schools, where many men were "tokens" for the first time in their lives. I explore the consequences of being a token when men are the minority group. Since the theory of tokenism is based on case studies of women in men's occupations, I argue that it has only limited applicability to the case of men. Discrimination is not a simple by-product of numbers: The social organization of work tends to benefit certain groups of workers over others, regardless of their proportional representation in an occupation. Consequently some groups (like women) suffer because of their minority status; other groups (like men) do not.

Chapter 5 looks at how well men are accepted by their colleagues, supervisors, and clients in the workplace, analyzing both the advantages and the disadvantages men encounter because of their gender. This chapter focuses on the occupational structure and workplace culture of these professions, showing how the "glass escalator" enhances men's careers *despite* their individual motivations.

Chapter 6, in contrast, focuses on individual motives. Using a feminist psychoanalytic approach, I explore the psychological conflicts faced by men doing "women's work" and their personal efforts to assert and maintain their masculinity. For the men in these professions, masculinity is contested terrain: The outside world considers them failures as men, while inside their professions they are rewarded because they are men. I examine the ways they negotiate the meanings of their masculinity, and actively constitute and manage their identity as men. Men in these traditionally female professions experience conflicts over the reproduction of masculinity in particularly heightened form, providing an excellent context for examining the psychological issues at stake in the reproduction of gender differences in organizations.

Chapter 7 considers the possibilities for ending occupational segregation and achieving economic equity between men and women. I argue that the policies designed to improve women's economic status in the labor force could have unintended consequences of furthering men's privileged status within the "women's professions." Achieving proportional balance of men and women in these fields could exacerbate gender hierarchy instead of eliminating it. Male privilege will survive workplace integration—unless radical changes are made *both* in the structural arrangement of workplace organizations *and* in the interests of men that underpin occupational segregation. The experiences of "men who do women's work" indicate just how entrenched these interests are, and how far we have yet to go before men and women achieve true economic equality.

2

The Rise and Fall of the "Women's Professions"

Prior to the American Civil War, it was not uncommon for nurses, teachers, and librarians to be men. (Social work did not exist as a separate occupation until the twentieth century.) Men performed most of the nursing tasks during the Revolutionary War; George Washington ordered the employment of women as nurses only if adequate numbers of male surgeon's mates could not be found.[1] In eighteenth-century America, any kind of scholarly learning was considered men's exclusive purview, making the few jobs in teaching and librarianship off-limits to women.[2] However, by 1900, these occupations had been completely redefined as "feminine" and "maternal," and hence suitable only for women. This "sex change" had extremely important consequences for men's careers—not all of them negative. Although women became the preferred employees, the supervisory positions in most cases were reserved "for men only."

In the twentieth century, these occupations have experienced trends toward a second "sex change." As each sought to achieve higher status and pay, their "feminine" and "maternal" connotations became a source of great concern. Leaders in each of these fields attempted to disassociate them from the ideology of domesticity and to redefine their work as essentially masculine. This second sex change is still under way: Men are currently being recruited as an explicit strategy to raise the status and pay of these occupations. The second part of this chapter explores the reasons for this peculiar strategy of "professionalization," focusing on its consequences for the men who work in these fields.

Such changes illustrate how assumptions about gender become embedded in organizational structures. In the nineteenth century, the engendering of these occupations was contested terrain: Forceful arguments were made to legitimize women's entry into these jobs. Struggles over the appropriate gender of nurses, teachers, librarians, and social workers continue today, with important consequences for the job opportunities available for both men and women.

Single Women and the Ideology of Domesticity

During the nineteenth century, the United States was gradually transformed from a rural farm economy to an urban, industrialized one. Industrialization took large numbers of white men and single women out of their households and into factories and artisan shops. White single women originally worked in the textile mills, producing the same types of goods that they had manufactured in their homes. Married women were left in their homes with their children, with fewer productive functions. The home gradually became identified with a retreat from the productive sphere, and a new ideology developed that defined women as essentially maternal and domestic.[3]

By the late nineteenth century, new immigrants from Europe replaced the native-born single women in the textile factories. No longer needed to perform productive functions at home, these women entered the newly established women's colleges and training institutes if their families could afford to send them. It was this group of women—single, white, native-born, and well-educated— that filled the burgeoning professions of teaching, nursing, librarianship, and social work.

These occupations greatly expanded during the second half of the nineteenth century. Public schools began proliferating in the 1820s, and other social service institutions—including public welfare agencies, hospitals, and libraries—rapidly developed in the later years of the century. Table 2 illustrates the enormous growth of these professions from 1870 to 1930. As the occupations expanded, so did the proportional representation of women in them.[4]

Ironically, women's increasing participation in these fields was not considered inconsistent with the ideology that defined women solely in terms of their domestic function. Advocates for professional women often justified women's employment in these areas as expressions of their "true" feminine, maternal natures. For example, women's entrance into teaching was defended on "maternal" grounds. At the beginning of the century, teaching was a predominantly male occupation. Women taught school only during the summer, when both male teachers and pupils were needed in the fields for harvesting. Women were believed incapable of instructing or disciplining male students during regular school sessions.[5] But in 1845, Horace Mann, the secretary of the Massachusetts

Table 2
*Number of People (in thousands) and Distribution
of Women Employed in Occupations, 1870–1930*

Profession	1870	1880	1890	1900	1910	1920	1930
Nursing	1	2	5	12	82	149	249
% women	95.8	95.2	91.7	93.6	92.9	96.3	98.1
Teaching[a]	128	226	345	443	599	762	1063
% women	66.0	67.9	71.0	73.5	80.0	83.9	81.0
Librarianship[b]	<1	—	—	—	7	15	30
% women	20.2	—	—	—	78.5	88.3	91.3
Social Work[c]	—	—	—	—	16	41	31
% women	—	—	—	—	55.7	66.0	78.7

SOURCE: U.S. Bureau of the Census, Sixteenth Census of the United States:
1940, *Comparative Occupation Statistics for the United States, 1870–1940.*
(Washington, D.C.: Government Printing Office, 1943).
[a]Teachers include elementary and secondary teachers.
[b]Figures for 1870 are from Anita R. Schiller, "Women in Librarianship," in *The
Role of Women in Librarianship*, ed. Kathleen Weibel and Kathleen M. Heim
(Phoenix, AZ: Oryx Press, 1979), p. 238. According to Schiller, there were 213
librarians in the U.S. in 1870. In 1880, librarians were classified in the Census
as "Authors, lecturers and literary persons," and in 1890 as "Authors and literary and scientific persons."
[c]From 1870 to 1900, social workers were included in the same category as
clergymen, religious workers, and recreation and group workers. Figures for
1910 and 1920 include social and welfare workers, and religious workers.
Nineteen thirty was the first year that social and welfare workers were
enumerated separately. (In 1930, the combined number of social, welfare, and
religious workers was 62,531.)

Board of Education, wrote in support of women teaching
in the normal schools:

Is not woman destined to conduct the rising generation, of both sexes, at least through all the primary
stages of education? Has not the Author of nature
pre-adapted her, by constitution, and faculty, and
temperament, for this noble work? What station of
beneficent labor can she aspire to, more honorable,

or more congenial to every pure and generous impulse?[6]

Likewise, Catherine Beecher, hailed by historians as the most important force in the transformation of teaching from a male to a female occupation,[7] argued in 1835 that motherhood and teaching were practically identical pursuits:

> Most happily, the education necessary to fit a woman to be a teacher is exactly the one that best fits her for that domestic relation she is primarily designed to fill.[8]

This same ideology justified women working in nursing, social work, and librarianship as well. When Florence Nightingale penned her famous (some would say notorious) line in 1860, "Every woman is a nurse," she was articulating the belief that women's preordained role as caretakers naturally suited them for nursing.[9] The first U.S. training schools for nurses, which opened in 1873, stressed the importance of "womanly character" in their pupils, connoting a moral, motherly devotion to duty.[10] The schools promised to make pupils "go forth better women, better equipped for the battle of life, whether to grace homes of their own or to become the temporary members of the homes of the suffering."[11]

Women's domesticity also justified their participation in social work. In the late nineteenth century, the "friendly visitor" movement, one of the precursors to modern-day social work, was seen as a transfer of women's domestic function from their own families to less fortunate ones.[12] The other major precursor, settlement work, was clothed in maternal language by Jane Addams, who called it "an expression of the great mother breast of our common humanity."[13] And E. E. Southard, the chief male supporter

of women's participation in psychiatric social work, justified that endeavor as appropriate for women because
they would, after all, really be engaged in solving family
problems.[14]

A woman's natural domesticity amply fitted her for
work in libraries. In 1889, the following advice was offered to library planners:

> Something may be said of the desirableness of mak-
> ing the library wear a pleasant and inviting look. The
> reading room offers perhaps the best opportunity for
> this. A reading-room lately seen has a bright carpet
> on the floor, low tables, and a few rocking-chairs
> scattered about; a cheerful, open fire on dull days,
> attractive pictures on the walls, and one can imagine
> a lady librarian filling the windows with plants. Such
> a room is a welcome in itself, and bids one come
> again.[15]

Women were also preferred because of their ability to
promote "quiet and order." A British librarian speaking
at an international library conference in Manchester, England, pointed out

> Their [women's] services in the reading-rooms set
> apart for boys are especially valuable, exercising a
> restraining influence over the lads, and conducing to
> quietness, order, and decorum.[16]

Furthermore, women's putative patience for accurate, tedious work made them ideal candidates for cataloging,
and their maternal inclinations suited them to work in
the children's collections, a library specialty that has been
almost exclusively female since its inception in 1900.[17]

Efforts to define these occupations as adequately feminine and maternal were crucial for paving the way for

the employment of a "respectable" class of white single women. Prior to the late nineteenth century, these occupations were of dubious social status. Teaching, a male-dominated occupation at the beginning of the nineteenth century, was considered a job of last resort, reserved for upwardly mobile (and therefore transient) men, or otherwise unemployable men. The stereotype reflected in Washington Irving's characterization of Ichabod Crane—an incompetent, eccentric outsider ridiculed by the community—stigmatized those men who tried to make teaching their lifelong endeavor. Florence Nightingale worked hard to dispel the stereotype that hospital nurses "were too old, too weak, too drunken, too dirty, too stolid, or too bad to do anything else." In the nineteenth century, the "librarian" conjured up an image of a dark-suited grumpy old man.[18] In each of these cases, parents had to be convinced that sending their daughters to work in these areas would not impugn the status and dignity of their families.[19]

Social work did not exist as a separate, identifiable occupation until the twentieth century, so there were no preconceived stereotypes preventing women from entering this field. The closest nineteenth century precedent to trained social workers were the "friendly visitors" who worked for charity organizations on a volunteer basis. These visitors were middle- and upper-class women who attempted to help the poor through moral uplift and domestic instruction.[20] Thus, when social work education was first introduced in 1898, the occupation already had been legitimated as an appropriate activity for relatively high status "ladies."

Nonwhite women were not recruited into these burgeoning professions. Heightening the social status and respectability of these occupations to make them appeal to middle-class white women meant excluding lower-class, black, and immigrant women. In nursing, for example, black women were rarely admitted to training schools. All nursing schools in the South excluded black women, while the schools in the North imposed severely restrictive quotas. Darlene Clark Hine gives the example of the New England Hospital for Women and Children in Boston which allowed only one black woman and one Jewish woman admission each year. As a result, only six black women graduated from this nurse training school by the close of the nineteenth century.[21]

The drive to attract a "higher status" female labor force resulted in racist exclusionary practices in the other occupations as well. In the early charity organizations, immigrants and members of the working class were notably absent among the "friendly visitors," paid officials, and directors.[22] And although black men and women taught in all-black schools in the South, they were often persecuted and forced to work underground. The U.S. census did not even count nonwhite teachers until 1930.[23] The first black librarians did not emerge until 1905 when an apprenticeship training program for blacks was established at the Louisville Free Public Library. This was the only program that trained black librarians until 1925, the year the first segregated black baccalaureate degree program opened.[24]

The tremendous energy devoted to making these occupations palatable to middle-class white women was ultimately motivated by demographic and economic factors. The carnage of the Civil War diminished the ratio of men to women in the eastern and southern states, and many of the men who survived the war moved westward seeking their fortunes in farming or mining.[25] Thus, women were encouraged to enter these occupations in part because there were not enough men around to fill them.

The other major incentive for hiring women was that they cost much less to employ than men. Teaching, nursing, social work, and librarianship were all tied to institutions that were funded by private donations or government support. Labor costs had to be kept down as much as possible, and well-educated women would work for a fraction of the salaries that "comparable" men commanded. Employers readily acknowledged this benefit of employing women. For example, in 1877, Justin Winsor, the first president of the American Library Association, bragged at an English conference of librarians:

> In American libraries, we set a high value on women's work. They soften our atmosphere, they lighten our labor, they are equal to our work, and for the money they cost—they are infinitely better than equivalent salaries will produce in the other sex.[26]

Single white women worked for lower wages than comparably educated white men because their employment options were far more limited. Aside from the four professions under consideration, the only occupations available to single women from the "respectable" classes were clerical and sales work—and women flocked to those jobs as well.[27] Nevertheless, advocates of hiring women into these professions at low wages insisted that women could be paid very little because they simply did not need a higher wage. Here the ideology of domesticity fit nicely with the economic incentives to pay women less. According to this ideology, women were only in these jobs to prepare for their future role as wives and mothers. They therefore were not supporting families on their incomes; indeed, they were expected to quit work once they were

summoned to their "true" calling. For example, in her effort to convince Congress to fund free teacher training
institutes for women, Catharine Beecher argued in 1853:

> To make education universal, it must be moderate
> in expense, and women can afford to teach for one
> half, or even less the salary which men would ask,
> because the female teacher has only to sustain her-
> self; she does not look forward to the duty of sup-
> porting a family, should she marry; nor has she the
> ambition to amass a fortune.[28]

The ideology of domesticity also justified paying wom-
en less by framing "women's work" in terms of maternal
duty and self-sacrifice. The woman working for feminine,
altruistic motives did not need "profane" money to reward her efforts. Melvil Dewey, a leading advocate for the
employment of women in libraries, recruited women looking for moral—not financial—reward:

> In the library profession, the best work will always
> be done on the moral plane. . . . The selfish consid-
> erations of reputation, or personal comfort, or emol-
> ument are all secondary. . . . There is absolutely no
> attraction for salary hunters.[29]

Susan Reverby argues that the nursing profession's own
stress on womanly duty gave hospitals carte blanche to
exploit their student nurses. In the late nineteenth century, some nursing leaders opposed hospitals' practice of
paying their student nurses, believing that women motivated by financial reward would not bring the high-
minded ideals of womanhood to their nursing practice.[30]
And, significantly, modern social work has its roots in the
unpaid volunteer work of relatively well-to-do women.
Thus, the ideology of domesticity provided ample justi-

fication for paying women lower wages (if any!), making single white women particularly attractive to employers.

Black women were cheaper to hire than white women, but the number of educated black women was far too meager to meet the growing demand for labor in these occupations (a result of their exclusion from training). Some institutions that were completely segregated— southern schools and hospitals, for example—did employ black women and men, but always at appreciably lower pay than white women received.[31] Blacks teaching in southern schools faced additional economic hardship because these schools were in session for a shorter period of time, sometimes for as little as three months per year.[32]

The white men who remained in these occupations were consistently paid higher salaries than the highest-paid women. In teaching, librarianship, and social work, men typically earned double the salaries of their female counterparts.[33] Alice Kessler-Harris has examined the different reasons for men's higher salaries during this period. She argues that in the nineteenth century, the wage structure for men reflected the relative "value of the job": The wage was a measure of the worth and importance of the work and what it produced. In contrast, she writes, "women's wages have traditionally been justified in terms of the needs of the worker. They have assumed the bare cost of subsistence, not the value of the job, as the appropriate measure of women's work." As a consequence, the male wage fostered high aspirations and achievement incentives; the female wage fostered dependence on the family for support.[34] Thus, on the one hand, the ideology of domesticity justified women's lower wages. The lower wages, in turn, fostered women's continued reliance on the family for economic support.

Over the period 1870–1930, the economic pressures

which led employers to hire women were exacerbated, forcing some organizations to reassess these differential pay scales. One-fifth of the nation's largest school systems eliminated their discriminatory policies by the first decades of the twentieth century.[35] In Memphis, for example, all teachers' salaries were lowered in 1878 to the women's levels of pay. Significantly, no male teachers were hired by the city in the subsequent school year.[36]

In New York City the elimination of differential pay scales for male and female teachers was more drawn out and embattled. Female teachers organized in 1907 to fight for "equal pay for equal work." According to Robert Doherty's fascinating history of this social movement, male teachers organized themselves into the "Male Elementary Teachers Association" to oppose this legislation. The male teachers defended discriminatory pay scales as in the best interest of men, children, *and women!* Men needed attractive salaries to keep them from pursuing lucrative alternative careers. Children (especially boys) needed high quality (and thus expensive) male teachers to provide role models in the classroom to keep them from becoming "feminized." And women needed low salaries, they argued, to draw them into marriage, thus lessening their chances of winding up among the "celibate class." Although their countercampaign against equal pay was ultimately unsuccessful, the male teachers did manage to win the support of high public officials (such as the mayor of New York City) as well as the editorial board of the *New York Times*, which promoted their cause.[37]

Lower salaries did not always result in the total diaspora of men from these four occupations, as was feared. Rather, the more likely scenario was for the "remaining" men to become administrators. In fact, as the number of administrative and supervisory jobs increased in these four professions, so did the likelihood of filling these positions with "men only."[38]

In education, for example, the introduction of graded schools in 1847 led to the proliferation of principalships and superintendent positions which were intended for men.[39] Thus, in Memphis, the year after instituting "equal pay" for male and female teachers, no male *teachers* were hired, but four male *principals* were hired by the school district.[40] Women were barred from joining the National Education Association at midcentury, another indication that their role in education was limited to classroom teaching—not teacher supervision.[41]

The same gender-based hierarchical division characterized nursing, social work, and librarianship as well. Florence Nightingale's philosophy placed nurses under the direct supervision and control of physicians. Nightingale encouraged doctors to "make the nurses obedient to them,"[42] thus forging the image of "the physician's hand" which has beleaguered nursing's efforts to establish professional autonomy ever since. Women's exclusion from medical education contributed to the sex segregation of hospital work: As nursing programs grew in number, the medical profession was busy closing those "special" programs that previously had trained female physicians, and establishing barriers to women's entrance into the remaining medical schools. Hospital nursing and medical social work—occupations under the direct supervision of male doctors—attracted many of the women who otherwise might have pursued medical educations.[43]

The few men who did receive nurse training for the most part attended "male only" schools, which were attached to insane asylums. These schools came under the auspices of the Medico-Psychological (later named American Psychiatric) Association. The nurses trained in these institutions were not allowed to become part of the American Nurses' Association until 1930. In fact, they were not even called "nurses." Instead, they were known as "attendants." Thus, during the period 1870–1930, it was extremely rare for any men to be employed in hospital nursing alongside female nurses, or among the higher ranks of the nursing hierarchy.[44]

In librarianship, where men made up a slightly larger proportion of the occupation, the high-paying directorships of major libraries were reserved for male librarians. Melvil Dewey, who recruited women to work in libraries for "moral" reasons, tempted men with the lure of high salaries and ample opportunities for advancement. In his essay, "Librarianship for College Men," he wrote:

> I rather hesitate to thrust the dollars and cents sign to the foreground but it makes if not a high, at least an insistent appeal.[45]

Men were preferred for administrative jobs even though women were cheaper to hire for a variety of reasons. First, women were deemed physically and temperamentally unsuited for the stress of administrative work. This position was articulated in a 1904 essay appearing in *Library Journal:*

> Women are quite generally acknowledged to work under a handicap because of a more delicate physique. This shows itself in less ability to carry calmly the heavy burdens of administrative responsibility, to endure continued mental strain in technical work or to stand for a long period.

According to the author, their feminine frailty made women inappropriate candidates for "the highest administrative positions in libraries," but amply qualified to head "small or medium sized libraries":

> It is quite generally conceded that in positions which do not involve the highest degree of executive or business ability but which require a certain "gracious hospitality," women as a class far surpass men.[46]

The ideology of domesticity which justified women's participation in these occupations thus worked to exclude them from the high-ranking positions. In teaching, women's maternal function, which gained them admission into the profession, excluded them from principalships. According to Charol Shakeshaft,

> School boards claimed they didn't want to invest time and money in workers with short-term commitments, a description often given to women who were expected to leave teaching for marriage. Typically, men didn't stay in teaching much longer than did women, but curiously the undependable label was applied only to women, thus limiting their opportunities for administrative posts.[47]

The expectation that women would quit teaching upon marriage and motherhood was formalized into law in several school districts. As late as 1942, 58 percent of the nation's school systems barred married women from teaching.[48]

Just as popular stereotypes of femininity excluded women from high posts, stereotypes of masculinity were used to defend the practice of only hiring men for administrative positions. Trustees, philanthropists, and politicians were believed to prefer business dealings with male administrators. A library trustee expressed this prefer-

ence at the 1892 meeting of the American Library
Association:

> My reason for preferring a man for the head of a
> library in a large city is not based on what may be
> called library *per se*. It is connected with the business
> side of the librarian's position. Unfortunately
> women are hedged about with rules of decorum and
> courtesy which somewhat interfere with their use-
> fulness in many relations in a municipal or a busi-
> ness community; with the trustees, for instance, who
> may . . . comprise men of rough or at least of down-
> right and positive character. A man's relations with
> such a board are freer and more likely to be influ-
> ential than a woman's, because he can talk right *at*
> them and *with* them, without offense on either side.
> He is usually accustomed to hasty and unfair criti-
> cism and knows how to meet it effectively. With the
> city government—especially the council who make
> appropriations—a man can work far more efficiently
> than a woman can. He can go out among them at
> their offices and stores, or in the City Hall corridor;
> can learn what influences are brought to bear on
> them, and so benefit the library in a score of ways
> closed to a woman. With the rougher class of the
> community, with laborers and artisans, a man, for
> obvious reasons, can do more effective work.[49]

School boards preferred men in the top positions for the
same reasons.[50] And Mary Richmond and Sophonisba
Breckinridge, two early leaders in social work, demurred
to male authority explicitly because they believed it essential for the success of public welfare projects and university departments that men be placed in charge. Men
brought greater status and authority to administrative
positions, so it was seen as in the best interest of the profession to place them in the most visible and powerful
positions.[51]

Even though men increasingly dominated the top administrative positions, the number of women entering these occupations continued to outstrip the number of men. The 1920s were peak years for proportional representation of women in each of these occupations. During this decade of relative economic affluence, educated men faced a wide array of occupational choices. Thus, the few men who were employed in teaching, social work, and librarianship generally found themselves at the top, or on their way up.[52]

The Great Depression of the 1930s had only limited effects on the gender composition of the rank-and-file members of these occupations. Generally, women managed to hold on to their jobs in librarianship, nursing, and social work. However, the number of women teachers and administrators declined over the decade. Men began to see these relatively secure, publicly financed jobs in a more favorable light, and according to Nancy Cott, employers took every opportunity to hire male teachers and administrators.[53]

By the 1930s, men were being welcomed into nursing, teaching, librarianship, and social work, particularly as each of them began to "professionalize." Several of the top leaders in these fields, attributing the relatively low pay, prestige, and lack of autonomy of their occupations to their nonprofessional or "semi-professional" status, advocated various strategies for "professionalization"; these included raising educational standards, formulating state licensing procedures, and, significantly, recruiting men.

Men and Professionalization in the Twentieth Century

The strategy of recruiting men to raise occupational status was first introduced at the turn of the century, but it has reemerged periodically throughout the twentieth century, reaching its height of popularity in the 1960s. In social work, for example, John Ehrenreich writes that advocates of professionalization have repeatedly seen the field's largely female composition as "a cause for concern rather than pride":

> Only by recruiting men into key positions in the field would social work gain in power and prestige, argued Mary Richmond and other social work leaders at the turn of the century; late fifties and early sixties writers had echoed their agreement.[54]

Social scientists are partly responsible for the popularity of this gender-based strategy for professionalization, although it is not clear that they intended to have this effect. In the 1950s and 1960s, eminent sociologists, including Talcott Parsons, William Goode, Harold Wilensky, Amitai Etzioni, and Peter Rossi, confidently proclaimed that professional status would forever elude these "semi-professionals." Writing in 1961, William Goode declared,

> Librarians, nurses, and social workers have spent much energy in trying to professionalize their occupations during the past several decades, but nursing will not become a profession, the other two have not yet become professions, and I am doubtful that the librarians will become full-fledged professionals.[55]

These sociologists devised elaborate explanations to account for these occupations' lack of professional status. They drew up lists of occupational criteria that characterized the "true" professions, and then "demonstrated" that the "semi-professions" failed to meet the criteria for professional status.

In a review of this literature, David Austin found that no two sociologists have come up with the same set of criteria, nor have any two ever agreed on which occupations should be labeled "professions." Nevertheless, many of the nurses, teachers, librarians, and social workers who read the sociologists' work—and cited them in their own scholarly journals—accepted these classification systems as objective, scientific "truth."[56]

Conspicuously absent from the lists of professional criteria was any reference to the sexual composition of the occupation. Of course, it is no coincidence that the "true" professions they used as models for their lists were almost exclusively male at the time (e.g., medicine, law, the clergy), in contrast to the overwhelmingly female "semi-professions." But these writers did not link the low esteem accorded to these occupations to society's sexist devaluation of women and the work they did. They did acknowledge that women predominated in these occupations, but they argued that this was because women were *drawn to* low-status occupations. Simpson and Simpson provide the classic statement of this position:

> A woman's primary attachment is to the family role; women are therefore less intrinsically committed to work than men and less likely to maintain a high level of specialized knowledge. Because their work motives are more utilitarian and less intrinsically task-oriented than those of men, they may require more [bureaucratic] control. Women's stronger competing attachments to their family roles and . . . to their clients make them less likely than men to develop colleague reference group orientations. For these reasons, and because they often share the general cultural norms that women should defer to men, women are more willing than men to accept the bu-

reaucratic controls imposed upon them . . . and less
likely to seek a genuinely professional status.[57]

The fact that women predominated in these occupations,
it was argued, signaled the jobs' low status since women
were not socialized to fit into truly professional occupations. Talcott Parsons, who believed that women were socialized to be "expressive," and men, "instrumental," thus
explained professional stratification:

> On higher levels typical feminine occupations are
> those of teacher, social worker, nurse, private sec-
> retary and entertainer. Such roles tend to have a
> prominent expressive component, and often to be
> "supportive" to masculine roles. Within the occupa-
> tional organization they are analogous to the wife-
> mother role in the family. It is much less common
> to find women in the "top executive" roles and the
> more specialized and "impersonal" technical roles.
> Even within professions we find comparable differ-
> entiations, e.g., in medicine women are heavily con-
> centrated in the two branches of pediatrics and psy-
> chiatry, while there are few women surgeons.[58]

Several of these writers noted that administrative and
supervisorial positions, the most "professional" roles
within the four occupations, were predominantly held by
men. Wilensky pointed out (with unmasked approval)
that young, ambitious men were increasingly entering the
"women's fields" on a fast track to the top.[59] Peter Rossi
urged librarianship, education, and social work to follow
the model of nursing and institutionalize a hierarchical
division of authority (along sex lines) so those at the top
could be duly recognized as true professionals:

> Much could be done to raise the status of the entire
> field[s] by making the division of labor as radical as

that accomplished in medicine where nursing is the female occupation and doctoring the male.[60]

This argument linking the achievement of professional status to a preponderance of men sparked recruiting drives to attract more men. As if to prove to sociologists that their occupations merited higher status, leaders in these fields began re-defining their work in ways that were meant to appeal to more "masculine" orientations. They stressed the impersonal, technical, and scholarly aspects of their work instead of the emotional and relational components in concerted drives to attract more men to their occupations.

In the 1960s, for example, the American Library Association consciously targeted men by issuing recruitment brochures with the titles, "The Librarian—Merchant of Ideas," and "The Librarian—Idea Consultant." Special libraries hired men with promises to place them "in the areas of administration, science and technology, and computer information systems."[61] The American Association of Elementary-Kindergarten-Nursery Educators unanimously approved a resolution in 1969 urging the recruitment of more male teachers in elementary classrooms to provide boys with "a male image."[62] The concern was repeatedly expressed that the next generation of males would be "feminized" unless greater numbers of "manly" men were brought into the lower grades:

Women teachers know almost nothing about boy games, and most couldn't care less. Typically the woman teacher is about as involved in the World Series as boys are in the score of *La Traviata*. This is not a trivial matter. Sports and games . . . are central to the boy personality. Much of a boy's life is spent playing sports, watching them, or talking about them. Thus this intense inner life of boys is given little chance for exposure in the academic classroom.[63]

Social workers, too, engaged in recruitment campaigns to attract "masculine" men to improve the professional standing of the occupation.[64] Even nurses turned to men to upgrade their nonprofessional status. In 1976, Bonnie Garvin wrote,

> A changing profession in a changing society needs individuals, males and females, who value the empirical, critical, and rational orientation. Recruiting men into nursing is one resource for this type of interest or value.[65]

This strategy continues to be promoted. Recruitment literature directed toward men still emphasizes traditionally masculine qualities. An advertisement showing a man teaching elementary school uses the slogan, "Reach for the Power. Teach." The Army Nurse Corps recruits men with the promise to give them "an edge on career growth," and shows a man pumping iron in his spare time. The Navy's recruitment brochure suggests that male nurses have administrative responsibility and the opportunity to work with high technology. (The female nurses in this advertisement are shown in supportive and more nurturing roles.) And the scholarly literature in these fields continues to look to men for the promise of raising the fields' professional status. The following, for example, was published in the *Journal of Nursing Education* in 1984:

> It is hypothesized that one of the reasons nursing has been a low-prestige, low-power profession for so long is that the typical nurse has not been assertive

enough to lead or support real innovations. Perhaps males will assist in this venture as they bring increased commitment and new personality characteristics into nursing.[66]

It is clear that this strategy of recruiting men as a panacea to remove barriers to professionalization was (and still is) based on a misreading of the sociologists' analyses. The sociologists had argued that these "semi-professions" were *inherently* low-status jobs. Women were concentrated in these fields, they argued, because of their weaker labor force commitment (due to their feminine socialization and their competing family responsibilities). The leaders in these occupations turned the argument on its head: If men who were clearly masculine were employed in these fields, they argued, then surely that would signify that they were "true professions," and the benefits of professionalization would soon follow.[67]

Recent advances in our understanding of the process of professionalization have exposed the folly in both of these views. Elliot Freidson has shown that there is no "formula" or set of objective criteria that determines professional status. Rather, professionalization is achieved through mustering the political power to institute a monopoly on a set of specialized, essential, and unique skills.[68] Nurses, teachers, social workers, and librarians certainly possess the requisite skills; what they lack is the political power to establish monopolies on their practice. This lack of power is linked to the general devaluation of women, and the work they do, in society. Indeed, sociologists have found it to be the case that cross-culturally, the work women do is of "lesser status"—regardless of the actual nature of the work. Thus, to cite a familiar example, medicine is female-dominated in Russia, yet it is considered a relatively "low status" occupation (whereas hospital administration—a male specialty—is not).[69] This insight eluded the sociologists writing in the 1950s and 1960s.

Nevertheless, their work was enormously influential within these four occupations. In addition to inspiring the recruitment drives to attract men, the sociologists' proclamations condemning the "semi-professions" to inferior status provoked an outpouring of research documenting women's failure to aspire to professionalism and encouraging women to become more like men. Several articles appeared in the 1960s and 1970s showing that men possessed greater ambition and more "professional" orientations than women. The following example is from a 1979 study of 335 male and 508 female nursing students:

> Men are not likely to staff the nursing profession in the same manner as women. Male interests and orientations are toward the "professionalizer" rather than the "traditionalizer" or "utilizer" type of nursing role. While the "utilizer" looks at nursing without long-term commitment—"it's a job"—and the "traditionalizer" longs for a return to the succoring posture of the Florence Nightingale era, the "professionalizer" relies on acquired knowledge, accumulated technical competency and a "limited partnership" rather than a servant relationship with the physician in providing health care and therapy.[70]

Women's failure to achieve preeminence in their occupations was attributed to their personality flaws—not to the institutionalized preference for men in administration. Women's underrepresentation on school boards was due to "the apathetic attitude of women teachers toward administrative appointments."[71] And in a 1970 article, women were blamed for their inferior positions in social work:

> Women are better practitioners than men because they are more likely to possess such essential qualities as nurturance, succorance and intuitiveness. These are all expressive qualities. On the other hand, excellence in social work practice may depend more on instrumental qualities, such as ability to evaluate, to plan and to implement plans. And men, rather than women, may be more likely to possess these and other instrumental qualities.[72]

In librarianship, the fact that women "tolerated" the male dominance of their occupation was taken as yet another sign of their weakness and submissiveness. Responding to an article charging librarianship with discrimination against women in hiring and promotions, John Cary wrote in 1971:

> The most puzzling and disturbing aspect of the library feminist's claims is understanding how this great majority of librarians—four out of every five—can be so held down by the small remaining percentage. This claim only strengthens the suspicion that despite what anyone says, women are more passive and less keenly professional than men.[73]

And in a 1985 article in *Library Trends*, women's concentration in low-level positions was attributed to their "inability to acquire and demonstrate power when applying for a position."[74]

Thus, in the 1970s and 1980s, women were told to disassociate themselves from precisely those characteristics that made them ideal candidates for these jobs in the 1870s. Those maternal and wifely qualities contained in the ideology of domesticity were now seen as professional liabilities, and women were urged to become more "like men." Not only were women's prospects for career advancement at stake; the "professional" status of these occupations depended on women disavowing their "feminine" attributes.[75]

Conclusion

Throughout the twentieth century, nursing, teaching, social work, and librarianship have been associated with "women's work," but there is nothing natural or inevitable about this connection. In the mid- to late-nineteenth century, white middle-class women were drawn into these occupations to make up for a growing scarcity of men, who previously had been employed in these areas. An ideology of domesticity developed which legitimated each of these fields as suitable occupations for "ladies" (thereby diminishing their suitability for men). Unlike factory work, these jobs were considered "clean," they required some refinement and education, and they were believed to enhance women's future domestic functions. They were also low paying. This fact was used to justify hiring middle-class women, who, it was argued, did not need money to support themselves and their families. Communities and social-service agencies lacked the resources to attract higher-paid males (although the better-paying supervisory positions were reserved for men), so they specifically recruited women to fill these new positions.

Although femininity and domesticity originally legitimized middle-class women's entry into nursing, teaching, librarianship, and social work, these very attributes stymied their "professionalization." The leaderships of these four occupations became increasingly concerned that their largely female composition condemned them to inferior social status, pay, and authority. In their efforts to "professionalize," these leaders led drives for greater male participation in these occupations, and appealed for the "masculine resocialization" of the women employed in these jobs. Thus, over the course of a mere 150 years, these occupations were transformed from "masculine" to "feminine," and back to "masculine" (at least according to those aspiring to professionalization).

The identification of certain tasks and jobs as "masculine" or "feminine" is thus extremely malleable. Jobs that are "masculine" at one time are "feminine" at others. Similarly, identical tasks can be male-identified in some occupations, and female-identified in others. As we have seen, female librarians were once lauded for their ability to discipline young boys, while female teachers were assumed incapable of performing the same task.

Although it is malleable, this ideology is nevertheless effective in constraining employment options for men and women. The definition of nursing, teaching, social work, and librarianship as "women's work" has framed men's participation in these fields over the past century, and it continues to do so today. Despite the recruitment drives of the 1960s and 1970s, there are very few men who are currently employed in these occupations, and those men who do work in these fields still occupy the best jobs. Gender differences may be an ideological fiction, but they have very real material consequences.

3

An Unconventional Career Choice

When asked, "What do you want to be when you grow up?" very few boys say they want to be nurses, teachers, librarians, or social workers. A 1970 survey of young adults found that fewer than 2 percent of the boys aspired to these occupations, in contrast to nearly 20 percent of the girls. High school boys consistently rank nursing their least likely occupational choice.[1]

Even the men who enter these professions did not aspire to them as children. A California teacher told me, "I was never going to be a teacher. My mother was a teacher and it was the last thing I wanted to do." The men in this study recalled far more conventional aspirations from their childhoods, as did this Arizona librarian:

> I like what I'm doing now, but I wouldn't as a five- or six-year-old kid—when I wanted to be a football player—I wouldn't have said, "Oh, I want to be a librarian!" [laughs] It's the sort of thing for people, when they're at a certain stage of their life, they want to switch gears.

Childhood aspirations are notoriously bad predictors of where adults end up working (otherwise there would be many more football players and ballerinas in the labor force).[2] However, studies have shown that children's occupational aspirations are as sex segregated as the work world itself. Boys and girls learn different occupational values and expectations from parents, school textbooks, guidance and vocational counselors, and the mass media, and this socialization is backed up by peer group pressure.[3] Children police each other, and ostracize those who do not conform to gender-appropriate behavior.[4] The one man I interviewed who always aspired to being a nurse recalled how he was taunted as a teenager:

> I think there's a stigma with nursing, that if you're a male and you're a nurse, you're gay. And a lot of adolescents, of course, when they're trying to decide what they're going to do with their life, they don't want that extra stigma on them. And that was very difficult in high school for me. People called me "Christina" instead of "Christopher" when I said I wanted to be a nurse. I'm sure it still goes on.

Arguably, boys face even more social disapproval than girls do for showing interest in the activities of the "opposite" sex: Being called a sissy, for example, is probably a worse insult than being called a tomboy. Little girls can now play with "Barbie" dolls outfitted as surgeons and jet pilots (as well as nurses), but there has been no equivalent change in boys' toys. Because the boy who plays girls' games is often stigmatized and even punished, it is not surprising that few respondents claimed any early interest in their present occupations.

In contrast, several of the women I interviewed recalled aspiring to their current professions very early in life.

This second grade teacher in Texas had fond memories of being in the second grade:

> I loved my teacher, and I wanted to be just like her. And all the extra material she had left over and stuff like that, I'd take home with me, and try to teach my little brother, using those little cards and things like that.

For the most part, the men in this study were already in college when they first considered entering their occupations. Even then, many remembered that they had negative stereotypes about these fields. Librarians described the ubiquitous stereotype of the "little old lady with a bun who shushes people all day," an image one man described as the "Maid Marian Librarian." Teaching carried the stereotype of being "tedious" and suitable only for those who failed in everything else. ("If you can't do, teach.") One California man thought a social worker was "someone who gives out food stamps for the county"; others imagined "Pollyanna do-gooders." And finally, nurses are women. This stereotype is so entrenched that children are confused at the prospect of a man in nursing. One Massachusetts man told me that when he explained to his six-year-old nephew that he was in school to learn how to be a nurse, his nephew asked him, "Does this mean you're going to be a girl?" With all of these stereotypes, it is not too surprising that so few men ever consider pursuing these careers.

Women entering these professions are also confronted with negative stereotypes. Increasingly, women are forced to defend their decision to enter nursing, librarianship, teaching, and social work, especially as more opportunities for women are opened up in the higher status "male" professions.[5] For example, a woman who left a career in music education to pursue librarianship described her friends' reactions:

> I still remember my conducting teacher saying she couldn't see me sitting behind a desk with books piled sky high for eight hours a day. I mean, that was her image and that was pretty much my image. And a lot of people teased me about the stereotype; that they couldn't picture me as a librarian, you know, with glasses and my hair pulled back in a bun, and my prim little clothes.

This negative reaction faced by many women in these professions does not constitute a stigma, however. The very integrity of their character is not called into question as it often is when men express interest in these fields. After all, there is still a sense that women in these occupations are fulfilling a feminine role, even if that is not how they see themselves. For instance, a social worker active in lesbian and feminist organizing told me that her choice of profession was supported "even by the conservative elements of my family," who imagined her in the role of "Suzy Socialworker." To her, this traditional aura of the profession acted as a "cover" for her radical perspective:

> One of the beauties of social work is that junior leaguers feel comfortable with social workers and so do farm activists. . . . Because social work is a feminized profession, it's not considered as threatening as some other professions that are not so dominated by females. . . . You can use it to your advantage, to have that perception of the benign, nice, friendly, helpful kind of social worker, which is sort of the image a whole lot of people have, you know.

Of course, the downside of conflating these professions with the "female role" in society is that some women feel pressured into these occupations. This Texas elementary school teacher, who resisted becoming a teacher because of her negative impressions of the field, explained how her parents nevertheless pushed her into it:

> We had a very traditional home. . . . It was the woman's role to grow up, get married, have children, and this would fit in perfectly. Since I was not married, it would give me something to do. [laughs] . . . [Teaching] seemed to be the perfect profession to go into that fit what everybody else wanted me to do.

Women entering these professions are still perceived as fulfilling a traditional female role (even if that is not how they see themselves), while men are seen as violating the traditional male role.

But this is not necessarily how the men see themselves. With few exceptions, the men I interviewed did not consider themselves "trailblazers" into nontraditional roles. Most men were drawn into their professions from prior job experiences. Several librarians, for example, had worked part-time in libraries to pay their way through college. Once there, they discovered they liked the work, and then decided to pursue it as a career. Several of the male nurses I interviewed had prior experience as military corpsmen or emergency medical technicians, positions that are usually supervised by registered nurses. To them, nursing seemed the next logical step up in the organizational hierarchy of medical work. Sometimes the initial work contact was more tangential. For example, one kindergarten teacher got his start in the profession photographing children in a preschool program.

Social and political concerns did motivate several of my respondents who were attracted to the "helping" or service orientation of these professions. One Native

American social worker claimed he was drawn to his profession because it enabled him to serve Indian people and enhance his community's autonomy from the federal government. Likewise, two gay men told me that concern about the AIDS epidemic inspired their original interest in nursing. One man left a career of more than twenty years in banking to enter nursing school after the experience of caring for a friend dying of AIDS convinced him that nursing was his true calling.

But many of those interviewed were not "driven" in their professional pursuits, and instead described themselves as directionless until friends or relatives stepped in with career advice. For example, one man who was an athlete in college, was encouraged by his tutor to consider taking courses in her major, social work. When I asked him how he envisioned his future career at the time, he said,

> I saw myself playing professional football. [laughs] And social work as an off-season back-up. But I didn't think it would be my main field of work.

The fact that social work is predominantly female did not concern him; in fact, he claimed he was unaware that men were in the minority until he began working. His primary identity was tied more closely to his hoped-for career in football, a quintessentially "masculine" pursuit.

This special education teacher described a similar trajectory into his profession:

> My roommate was an education major, and he said there was this class that you would get an *A* in without doing any homework. . . . I was very reluctant to take any courses in the education department. . . . I just hated the thought of teaching. But he said this one course . . . , you would go out to a school, you

> sit in the back of the room, you do observation, that's
> all you have to do. So, I did that. I got sent to a first
> grade classroom, and fell in love with the miniature
> furniture and the little kids [laughs] and basically . . .
> I was pretty much hooked after that.

In his case, the original contact with teaching came on
the advice of a male friend. This turned out to be a crucial
factor in his decision making: He mentioned that he felt
comfortable pursuing a career in education only because
there were "two or three or four other guys going into it."
Once again, he had no desire to break down gender distinctions with his occupational choice, nor did he consider himself "nontraditional." In fact, the predominantly
female composition of the teaching field caused him
some trepidation precisely because he did not want to
appear unmanly.

For some of my respondents, the move into their current professions was a midlife career change. One man,
who was "burned out" in his career as a lawyer, became
a school band director, a job he eventually tired of as well:

> I couldn't see myself being a band director from now
> on. . . . It's kind of like coaching; it's more or less for
> younger men. . . . You know, generally men don't
> stay in that forever. They go into administration,
> some other level of school work, or sell insurance or
> real estate or whatever. They get out. . . . So I
> couldn't see myself doing it from now on. In fact, I
> was getting a little burned out, to tell you the truth.
> . . . So I was looking around for something else that
> I could do in the school business, and I don't want
> to become a principal because I think they have their
> own headaches that I don't really want to mess with.
> And I thought about counseling at one time. But
> then, my wife is a school librarian, and I've been

helping her off and on through the years and it looked pretty attractive to me, so I decided, "Well, I'll just go into school library work."

This hulking, yet extremely affable man, exuded total confidence about his work as an elementary school librarian. Without flinching, he declared, "I love little bitty kids. . . . They're just as cute as bugs' ears." He had absolutely no conception of himself as a gender renegade in his occupational choice. Those men I interviewed who had previous careers in male-dominated fields, like this man did, seemed completely unconcerned about the predominantly female composition of their new occupations. In a sense, they had already "proven" their masculine credentials in their previous work, which enabled them to relax and enjoy work closer to their true calling. And, as this particular interview excerpt suggests, having a supportive family also facilitates the transition into "women's work."

Family influences were also important in the case of men in dual-career relationships. Two of the men I interviewed (one librarian and one nurse) were married to academic women. They had self-consciously chosen their professions for the potential geographic mobility they offered. As the librarian put it, "If you're a female academic, your husband has to do something, and a librarian is one [option]. It's a lot easier than being two academics."

Several female respondents mentioned this sort of family obligation as an important factor leading them to their present careers. Many said they chose their professions because they were able to arrange their childbearing and child rearing around their work responsibilities. For example, one woman told me she entered teaching so that she could have "my weekends and summers off" to spend time with her own children.

There is some dispute among sociologists about whether or not women in general "choose" occupations which permit them to assume primary responsibility for housework and childcare. Paula England, for example, found that women employed in predominantly female occupations are no more likely to take periodic breaks from the labor force than other employed women.[6] On the other hand, Sue Berryman and Linda Waite found that young women who anticipated that they would bear primary household and childcare responsibilities in their families as adults are likely to aspire to predominantly female occupations.[7] My sense is that both findings are probably correct. That is, women who anticipate that they will be in traditional family settings (with primary responsibility for the house and child care) probably do select predominantly female professions more readily, believing them to be more accommodating to their future needs. Women who aspire to nontraditional career choices probably are not aware of the problems besetting women who try to combine such jobs with family responsibilities. Recent studies suggest that young women today are convinced that they can "have it all" (the "male" career and the mother role); that often becomes impossible, however, once they enter the labor force.[8] Thus, many women must take time out of the labor force to manage their home lives, a circumstance they did not anticipate at the outset of their careers.

In general, men are still far less likely than women to arrange their work lives around their family responsibilities or to drop out of the labor force temporarily to care for the house and family. In 1990, for example, fewer than 1 percent of men, aged sixteen and over, spent their time "keeping house" according to the U.S. Bureau of Labor Statistics. In contrast, over 25 percent of women were so occupied.[9] Thus, it is not surprising that very few men in my sample mentioned family responsibilities as a motivation behind their decisions to enter these occupations. Although I did talk to some men who appreciated that their professions permitted spending more time with family and friends compared to other "high-powered" professions, this attribute did not enter into their original motivations to enter these occupations as it did for many of the women I interviewed.

Friends or relatives often introduced the idea of these professions to the men I interviewed, but time and money concerns eventually clinched their decisions to enter their fields. Compared to the alternatives they were considering, their ultimate choices of careers promised a quicker payoff with a lower initial investment in "human capital." This Texas man recounted the decision-making process that led him to nursing:

> I was twenty-two years old and I had about forty hours of college, none of which was any good for anything other than it was really interesting. And I was trying to decide. And I was at that time in my life where I needed to get a job, and I made a decision to go into nursing.
>
> [CW: Why nursing? Was there somebody in your family that is a nurse, or did you know people who were nurses?]
>
> No. I knew a couple of medics, the people who were in my circle of friends, men who had either become physicians' assistants or nurses, and that field was accepting men. Some of them had been in Vietnam as medics, and they had made the decision to go into nursing. And it sounded like an interesting field. And that was a time of economic depression—during Nixon's second term—and the U.S. was in a fairly

severe depression, around '72–'73. And there was a lot of question about jobs. I mean, it was even worse than today. . . . And nursing was one of the professions at that time that clearly needed more people and appeared to have a lot of stability. It required a relative minimum amount of preparation. . . . It needed less preparation than becoming a physician—I was not interested in going to school for eight years—that did not interest me.

This illustrates the importance of male contacts to legitimize men's entrance into these professions. It also indicates that job availability and stability were important factors attracting men to these professions. Those men who came of age in the late 1960s and early 1970s in particular perceived plentiful opportunities awaiting them in these fields (owing to the contemporary political climate of support for public welfare spending). Men coming of age in the 1980s were less sanguine about their job prospects (except in nursing). But their chosen professions presented better job prospects than their alternatives, as in the case of this California librarian:

[CW: When did you first become interested in becoming a librarian?]

Not until very soon before I went into library school. I hadn't thought about it at all before that.

[CW: What happened that you considered going into it?]

A friend of mine who went to the same college I went to, went to library school the year before I did. He indicated it was something I might think about when I was expressing some negative thoughts about continuing on [and getting my Ph.D.] in history.

[CW: What was it that kept you from being overly enthusiastic about that possibility?]

A number of things. The thought that it was very hard to get an appointment at that time for Ph.D.'s in history. It costs money—although I had scholarships, it still costs. And I was a little disappointed about some of the arguments that historians were having with each other, and faculty members were having with each other. . . . I thought I would take a break from history and see if I liked something else. And then I never went back.

In his case, his history professors supported his decision to leave:

I was told by a professor I had at the college I went to that it was a good thing to do, go to library school, even though I was doing really well in history. He was dissatisfied. He knew if he had it to do over again, he wouldn't get a Ph.D. in history, and he had a good job. And he said it was something you could always fall back on if you wanted to in the future. It increases your options. He didn't really want to see me leave history, but it wasn't a bad thing to do.

These excerpts suggest that for some men, traditionally female fields were cheaper and more reliable alternatives to careers in predominantly male fields (e.g., medicine, academia). These particular men did not see themselves as making untraditional career moves; rather, a cost-benefit analysis convinced them that nursing and librarianship were reasonable substitutes for the more "masculine" professions they also considered. The fact that their contacts were male in both cases was also significant in clearing their career paths: Their male mentors legitimized these occupations for them by reassuring them that their gender would not stigmatize them.

Thus, most of the men I interviewed did not view their occupational choices as inconsistent or contrary to their masculine identities. They did not perceive themselves as "trailblazers," nor did they see their occupational choices as repudiations of the conventional male role in our society. That these fields are predominantly female was of some concern to many of these men, but their choices were ultimately legitimized by the encouragement of friends or family members who implicitly reassured them they would not be typecast as feminine by entering these occupations.

For many of the men I interviewed, this message that these occupations were consistent with masculinity was voiced only subtly and in passing, as in these last two examples. But in some cases, men explicitly defended their occupational choices as consistent with traditional masculine ambitions:

> [CW: Did it ever concern you when you were making the decision to enter nursing school, the fact that it is a female-dominated profession?]
>
> Not really. I never saw myself working on the floor. I saw myself pretty much going into administration, just getting the background and then getting a job someplace as a supervisor, and then working, getting up into administration.

Certain specialties within nursing, such as jobs in administration, are considered more legitimate for men and so do not pose a challenge to conventional concepts of masculinity. This Arizona public librarian also had definite ideas about more or less appropriate roles for men in his profession:

> I never really viewed [librarianship as female-dominated]. . . . It would be real unusual to find a male children's librarian. To me, then you would be really going against the grain. . . . But I think working with adults in reference is not unusual. . . . If you go to a university setting or a larger public library, I don't think people find it surprising that a male librarian would be helping them.

Because the specialties they chose were considered within their professions as more appropriate for men, many of the men I interviewed did not view their career choices as "nontraditional" at all.

I interviewed very few men who considered their occupational choices as an effort to break down gender distinctions. Nevertheless, they still faced social pressure to justify their career pursuits in stereotypically masculine ways. For example, even though this man viewed his occupational choice of elementary school teaching as drawing on his "feminine qualities," others did not see it that way:

> [My father's] first reaction was, "Well, that's a good start, and eventually, you know, you'll be able to be a principal, maybe start your own school." So that's where he was headed. He had a little more ambition than I had in mind. And every time I talked to him, his comments were always, "You still like it?" [laughs] "You still doing it?" . . . He would probably like it better if I was head of the school.

This teacher's father framed his son's interest in elementary school teaching as a stepping stone to more "masculine" jobs, despite the teacher's own definition of the situation.

But for the most part, the men I interviewed did not

conceive of their career choices as rejections of the traditional male roles in society, or as incompatible with their masculinity. This is another example of the extreme malleability of gender. Chapter 2 discussed how the definition of these occupations as "women's work" changed historically. Jobs typecast as masculine at one time are considered feminine at another, depending on which sex is predominantly engaged in the occupation. This same process occurs on the individual level. As this chapter has indicated, men often redefine their position in these jobs as masculine to legitimize their entrance into them. Most of the men I interviewed did not see their presence as challenging the prevailing cultural view of these occupations as feminine. Indeed, they often did not become aware of how untraditional their occupational aspirations were until they began their professional training. Entering professional schools, where men are greatly outnumbered by women, forced these men to come to terms with their "token" status. The next chapter examines these experiences and the consequences of tokenism—when men are the tokens.

4

Token Men in Training

When women first integrated male professional schools, stories of discrimination and harassment were legion. Cynthia Fuchs Epstein describes the extreme sexism encountered by the first women law students in the 1960s. During "ladies' days," women students would be forced to come to the front of the class where they were asked to recite answers to questions on "embarrassing" topics, typically ones involving family relationships or criminal sexual practices. If the women stumbled in their answers, they would be harangued with comments such as "Better go back to the kitchen." Reflecting on her observations, Epstein writes,

> Many a man feels diminished when a woman does better than he; and in law school, which is so evaluative and where grades count for so much, it is not surprising to find women the butt of antagonism. Furthermore, the women may feel especially vulnerable and uneasy on finding just how competitive they

really are and how resentful of this others seem to be.[1]

Similar experiences have been related by the first women to enter medical schools and the military academies.[2]

To make sense out of men's hostile reactions to the integration of women, sociologists developed a theory of tokenism. Rosabeth Moss Kanter, one of the leading theorists of tokenism, argued that the members of any social group will be discriminated against and marginalized if their group makes up less than 15 percent of an organization. In other words, she argued that the hostility encountered by women in "male jobs" was due to their numerical rarity. She predicted that with increasing proportions of women, this hostility would diminish.[3] According to Kanter, tokenism leads to discrimination and underachievement for several reasons. First, because tokens are visible—they readily stand out in a crowd—they experience extreme pressure to perform well, which is psychologically taxing, and thus tends to impede successful performance. Furthermore, members of the dominant group (called "dominants") often resent the extra attention tokens receive, interpreting it as unwarranted favoritism. Dominants view tokens as threatening to their culture, so they constantly subject the tokens to exaggerated displays of this culture, remind them of their difference, isolate them, and pressure them to accommodate and accept their dominant culture. Finally, tokens are subject to stereotyping. They are usually cast into peripheral roles that conflict with the demands of the organization. In her original and classic study of token female executives, Kanter found that these women were often typecast by the men as "mothers," "seductresses," "pets," or "iron maidens." These roles marginalize women because they define them in terms of their gender—not their relevant work skills.

This theory of tokenism is "gender-neutral"—it is meant to apply to both men and women whenever they constitute a numerical minority. However, most of the sociological literature on tokenism has focused on women in men's organizations, and has emphasized the negative consequences of numerical rarity for women's careers.[4] But what happens when men are the tokens?

Men in Women's Professional Schools

Substantial educational preparation is required to enter any of the "women's professions." To become a professional social worker or a librarian requires a master's degree. Elementary school teaching requires certification at the bachelor's degree level. Nursing recognizes three distinct educational tracks for entry-level practice: A registered nurse (RN) credential can be obtained through a three-year diploma program, a two-year associate degree program, or a four-year baccalaureate program. Additionally, a few master's level programs for entry-level certification have been developed in recent years.[5]

Kanter claimed that the effects of tokenism were most pronounced when the minority group consisted of approximately 15 percent of the total membership of an organization. Such is the case in all four professional schools, as shown in table 3. In 1988 men received 7 percent of all associate degrees and 5 percent of all baccalaureate degrees conferred in nursing, and about one-fifth of all master's degrees in library science and social work. Nearly a quarter of all graduates in education were men; however, fewer than 8 percent of the graduates in elementary education were men.

Table 3
*Number of Entry-Level Professional Degrees
Conferred, and Percentage Received by Men, by Field
of Study, 1987–1988*

Field of Study	Total	% Men
Nursing		
Associate degree	36,310	7.0
Bachelor's degree	31,567	5.1
Elementary Education		
Bachelor's degree	39,440	7.2
Social Work		
Master's degree	9,344	18.6
Librarianship		
Master's degree	3,713	21.3

SOURCE: National Center for Education Statistics, *Digest of Education Statistics, 1990* (Washington, D.C.: Government Printing Office, 1991), tables 223 and 224, pp. 235–43.

The proportions of men in these professional schools vary greatly from year to year, and from school to school. It was not unusual for my respondents to describe being one of only a handful of men in their programs. Many of the experiences common to female tokens were related by the men in this study. For example, being in a numerical minority meant that the men "stood out" in class and received more than their fair share of attention. One social work student who has "never had a class where there have been more than two males," noticed that "when I'm not there [in class], it really sticks out. Professors take attendance on me. They know when I'm not around." This "heightened visibility" was not experienced as discriminatory, however. Men described their professors as extremely supportive, even to the point of being overly solicitous, as recalled by this elementary school teacher:

I remember one old professor. She was past retire-
ment age. She was mean to all the women in the
courses. [laughs] I didn't particularly like her, so . . .
I stayed in the back of the room. . . . She always
raved excessively about all the projects that I turned
in, which . . . were good projects, but they weren't
that great.

Several men recalled that male professors were especially supportive during their professional training. The
faculty in these professional schools are far more "gender
balanced" than the rest of the profession (with the exception of nursing). Nearly half of all full-time faculty members in librarianship and social work are men, and over
60 percent of all professors of education are men. (Men
make up only 3 percent of all nursing faculty.)[6]

Many of the men in this study were sought out by male
faculty and explicitly encouraged *because they were men.*
One man recalled a male elementary education professor
who "tended to give me a lot more pats on the back than
. . . my female counterparts." A librarian described his
mentors in college:

The two people I was most friendly with were the
Associate Dean [male], and a man by the name of
Dr. Anderson. He taught fine printing. . . . As it happened, both of these people were subsequently important to me. Dr. Anderson lent me some money to
finance my move across the country after I got my
job.

Some men developed extremely close friendships with
their male teachers that extended into their private lives.
For example, a Texas librarian described an unusually
intimate association with two male professors in graduate school:

I can remember a lot of times in the classroom there would be discussions about a particular topic or issue, and the conversation would spill over into their office hours, after the class was over. And even though there were . . . a couple of the other women that had been in on the discussion, they weren't there. And I don't know if that was preferential or not. . . . It certainly carried over into personal life as well. Not just at the school and that sort of thing. I mean, we would get together for dinner. . . .

These professors explicitly encouraged him because he was male:

[CW: Did they ever offer you explicit words of encouragement about being in the profession by virtue of the fact that you were male?]

Definitely. On several occasions. Yeah. Both of these guys, for sure, including the Dean who was male also. And it's an interesting point that you bring up because it was, oftentimes, kind of in a sign, you know. It wasn't in the classroom, and it wasn't in front of the group, or if we were in the student lounge or something like that. It was . . . if it was just myself or maybe another one of the guys, you know, and just talking in the office. It's like . . . you know, kind of an opening-up and saying, "You know, you are really lucky that you're in the profession because you'll really go to the top real quick, and you'll be able to make real definite improvements and changes. And you'll have a real influence," and all this sort of thing. I mean, really, I can remember several times.

Other men reported a similar degree of closeness with their professors. A Texas psychotherapist recalled his relationships with his male professors in social work school:

> I made it a point to make a golfing buddy with one of the guys that was in administration. He and I played golf a lot. He was the guy who kind of ran the research training, the research part of the master's program. Then there was a sociologist who ran the other part of the research program. He and I developed a good friendship.

As these quotes imply, many of these men's close relationships with male faculty were subsequently very important in promoting their career development.

Relations with female faculty seemed more strained, according to the men's accounts. Although some men had female mentors in college, several described conflicts with individual women professors over grades, classroom climate, and personalities. Often these difficulties were attributed to the individual woman's inability to accept men's presence in "their" professions. For example, one nurse described an instructor who flunked him his senior year for "doing ridiculous things she wouldn't have written a female up for," such as breaking sterile technique by putting his hands in his pockets. He was convinced "she had something against me as a male" because she was "a dyke or something," so he hired a lawyer, and with the support of a male instructor, he eventually gained readmission to the course and was able to re-take it with another instructor.

There were other, more minor examples of conflict with female professors. A couple of the men perceived that they were "threatening" to some of their professors because they tended to be the most outspoken students in class (in contrast to their "meeker" female peers), and suffered retaliation for expressing their views too freely. One social work student was frustrated at the use of "sexist" examples in class:

> With more males there might be more of a sensitivity to males. . . . I noticed in class . . . last Monday we were talking about some hypothetical cases, males were always being cast as the hard guys. One case we were talking about, just making it up out of thin air, a woman was in an abusive relationship. The other case we were talking about, also making it up out of thin air, the male of the family was a substance abuser. Why is that? Why was that happening? I didn't comment on it at the time.

Generally, however, the few examples of discrimination described by the men in this study were far outweighed by the positive reinforcement they received from other instructors. In contrast to female tokens in professional schools, men are generally protected from discrimination and harassment by powerful faculty members—either male or female—who want to see more men enter and succeed in their professions. It is, in fact, common for schools of social work, librarianship, and education to be headed by male deans or directors. (This is still exceptional in the case of nursing.) These individuals can intervene or provide guidance to the student who is experiencing the discrimination. Women in the "male" professional schools usually lack same-sex role models or powerful mentors.

Furthermore, some men felt that they were the ones who were prejudiced against their female instructors, not vice versa. For example, a Texas librarian described one professor whom he particularly disliked:

> Maybe this is my way of being sexist, I don't know. . . . I guess we tend to stereotype people in profes-

sions; I mean the way they look and their behavior, that sort of thing. And this one professor in particular . . . seemed to have the appearance and the mannerisms of what one would consider the stereotypical librarian, right? She literally, of course, had the bun in her hair, and looked a little dowdy and looked older than probably she really was and talked in a real, low, quiet voice and that sort of thing. And I know it's terrible . . . , but at the time, I guess maybe I felt like . . . I mean, how can I have any respect for somebody that seemed to be the stereotype librarian? But I guess seeing some of the male professors I felt like, "Well, you know, the profession obviously is not all stereotypes," and . . . there are men in the profession, too, and they can be as intellectual and dynamic as anybody else.

Being a numerical dominant does not necessarily protect women from discrimination and harassment: Women professors can be the targets of sexism, even from structurally "powerless" male students.[7] In this case, the "token" male marginalized the "dominant" female through stereotyping and emphasizing difference from the token male culture. Because masculinity is more highly regarded than femininity in our culture, it behooves men to emphasize their difference by disassociating—and condemning—the women in their professions, even if the women are in more powerful positions. Men take their gender and all its attendant privileges with them when they enter these professions.

The troubles described in relating to some female faculty members were not present in their rapport with their fellow students. The men described very amiable, congenial relationships with their female peers. One man who attended nursing school in Philadelphia recalled,

"You get a lot of support from the other people in the class, the other girls. I had a great time in nursing school. I'd do it again." And a Texas man who returned to graduate school at age thirty-eight to earn his school librarianship credential—he was the only man in this specialty in his program—described the integration he experienced:

> There were a group of us . . . that kind of got together and ended up running the whole Graduate Library Student Organization. We printed the paper, and I was elected as advisor to the Faculty Council. . . . We organized the softball team, and we were all from different [specialties]. . . .We just enjoyed the heck out of being with each other.

Some men described their dating relationships with their female peers in college. For others, however, their fantasies of being surrounded by available and eager single women never panned out:

> [CW: Do you think you were accepted by your female colleagues?]
>
> Oh yeah.
>
> [CW: Did you go out partying with them?]
>
> Well, that was a problem. I kind of envisioned that's the way it was going to be, you know. Part of me thought, "Oh, this is great, a man going into this field [elementary school teaching]. There are going to be a lot of single women. This is going to be fun." It ended up that that wasn't the case at all. Most of them were . . . either married or already connected to someone.

A nurse in Massachusetts, who attended a diploma program which required residence at the hospital where he worked, was the only man in his dormitory which housed fifty students. He recalled,

> It became like having forty or fifty sisters. You'd walk down the hall, half awake, heading to the showers which were all individual cubicles type of deal, but you'd walk in and . . . three or four women would be walking out of their cubicles in their bathrobes saying, "Hi, how are you doing?" It was very relaxed, I have to say that, but it was sort of comical to look back on it in hindsight.

The hazing and harassment described by many women who enter formerly all-male educational institutions were entirely missing from these men's accounts. There was only one example of sexual intimidation in my interviews—and this from a man who felt *his* presence was intimating to the women students. He attended the librarianship program at a college where the undergraduate student body was exclusively female. He said,

> I recall many times feeling really out of place there, just being there physically was like, "I'm here in this place and it's not natural, normal." Sometimes even uncomfortable.

> [CW: Was there something institutionalized that made you feel uncomfortable?]

> No, more it was just the community. . . . Me being a man and finding myself in this place and being . . . say, being in the corridors and wandering around or in the cafeteria, and there being an overwhelmingly female population who would regard my presence as an intrusion or with a little bit of intimidation. A little woman finding herself in a corridor with a male my size can be . . . intimidated and find that a threatening thing. And being the object of someone else's

paranoia is not necessarily a lot of fun. It's like, "Oh, my God, what's this man doing here?"

This account was very unique, but it suggests that women's sexual vulnerability is not diminished by their numerical dominance. Men not only take gender privilege with them into these predominantly female occupations; they also take sexual power (notwithstanding any fantasies about being sexually overpowered by women).

Many women in this study corroborated the men's sense that they were welcome by their female peers in professional school. An elementary school teacher recalled that "everybody wanted to have a man in [their] classroom." When I asked if that "everybody" included the female students, she said, "Yes, absolutely, because everyone felt it was really good to have men who were going to want to be elementary school teachers." And a California social worker felt that the men in her program "got more attention from their [female] peers. The heterosexual and bisexual women were just thrilled to be around male energy, which is understandable."

The one source of strain that was mentioned on occasion was the perceived tendency of some men to monopolize classroom discussion. A female social worker enrolled in a master's program in Massachusetts described "one man in particular I keep remembering in my class, who attempted to monopolize conversation, and was shot down and became a pretty big scapegoat in that class." A social work instructor described a similar phenomenon, but she argued that women were complicit in giving men the opportunity to dominate the classroom:

I think that many women are inhibited in their verbal responses when men are present who otherwise may have made comments and so forth, which creates a climate, sometimes, that encourages men to speak. Thus, sort of, not very consciously, but catering to the men in the group. I am not like that, but I know a lot of women who are like that. . . . So I think when [the men in class] did speak—partly because of that rarity factor—there may have been a little bit more weight attached to their speaking.

According to this respondent, the heightened visibility of the male token is not resented by the female students as a form of favoritism—which is in contrast to the experience of female tokens. Rather, women in the class seem to defer to men, again suggesting that men bring "gender privilege" with them even when they are the tokens.

Several men described themselves as outspoken in class. The instructors I interviewed indicated that men were generally among the most vocal students in their classes. Thus it is not surprising that some might encounter antagonism from female students for dominating the classroom. Some men, however, demonstrated sensitivity to the sexual politics of the classroom. For instance, this Massachusetts social worker, who attended graduate school in 1973 when "women's liberation was . . . in the air," described taking a "strategic back seat" during class discussion. This can be interpreted as an example of the dominant group asserting its cultural norms against the presupposed values of the token. But when asked if he felt ostracized or antagonized by his female peers, he said,

[It was] sort of an impersonal antagonism when it existed. I remember not taking it personally, but there were some women, certainly angry, [who stated], "Women are the center focus here. This is our era, our program, more so than it is for you." And so I never felt personally affronted.

[CW: Were you ever shut down in class or anything like that when you were talking?]

Some memory of that, a little. But again, the person who would do that wasn't in full grip of themselves. So . . . you're only bringing it back by asking. It wasn't like a trauma, like being assaulted in class. . . . But it just reminded you that you needed your time and you needed to find the male colleagues.

Being around mostly women all the time was a source of discomfort for some, who sought out friendships with the few male peers in their classes. A student nurse in California explained,

Men have a different perspective, there's no doubt about it. I treasure the times when Phil and I just sat around and let off steam. I'm surrounded by women, and the times when I can hang out with men feel real good to me. And it's not just a matter of letting your hair down and talking about women and being dirty. We do that. But there's also just a different perspective.

The sense from these men was not that they were seeking solace with men due to being isolated or ostracized by their female peers. Rather, these men sought out others as a sort of refuge or "refueling" in masculinity. Particularly in nursing, where the symbols of the profession are so female-identified, the men often felt compelled to develop their own rituals and symbols. For example, in some nursing programs, the traditional nursing cap banded with a special color is the symbol of the school's graduate nurse. Because men never wear the traditional nursing cap, they can feel excluded from their school's pomp and circumstance. One man described his graduation-day antics to carve a "male niche" for himself and his male friend in the capping ceremony:

> A friend of mine has a clothing store. So I went down and got two white golf caps and I got my mother to sew on black bands, the thin ones that the seniors wore. . . . I kept threatening the director of nursing that we were going to wear our caps to graduation. . . . At graduation . . . I was class president so I had to give a speech, so when I went up on the stage to give my speech, I had hidden my cap. . . . It was too late, they couldn't stop the ceremony—I wore it. When Al got his diploma, he went over to where he hid his and put it on. So we disrupted things a lot.

Clearly, the "dominant's" culture in nursing sometimes excludes men. But the token men in this case were not forced to assimilate or accommodate that culture, which is what commonly happens to women. Rather, they were given the opportunity to develop their own cultural norms, without becoming marginalized. While it is quite possible that this student angered his instructors during the graduation ceremony, it is significant that he was *class president*. The challenge he represented to the "dominant's" culture was accommodated; indeed, he asserted and even exaggerated his difference from the dominant group, while maintaining an important role in the group.

Conclusion

The theory of token discrimination was developed using evidence from token women's experience of harassment and marginality in "men's" occupations. When men are in the minority, they do not experience the same negative effects of tokenism. For some, their numerical rarity is perceived as benign, if not beneficial, to their careers. Women in general seem to welcome men into "their" occupations, or, at the very least, there is little evidence that they establish roadblocks to derail or even marginalize men's careers. And because masculinity is more highly valued than femininity even in these predominantly female occupations, token men highlight their distinctiveness from the female majority.

The workplace is not gender-neutral, so our theories of occupational segregation should not be gender-neutral (like the theory of tokenism). Men take their gender privilege and sexual power with them into the token situation, making the effects of tokenism radically asymmetrical for men and women.[8] Numerical underrepresentation per se does not predetermine the success or failure of an individual: The relative social status of the individual is far more crucial.

Men are accepted and even encouraged in professional school because they are men. The next chapter examines how their token status also translates into material advantages once they enter the labor force.

5

Riding the Glass Escalator

Men earn more money than women in every occupation—even in predominantly female jobs (with the possible exceptions of fashion modeling and prostitution).[1] Table 4 shows that men outearn women in teaching, librarianship, and social work; their salaries in nursing are virtually identical. The ratios between women's and men's earnings in these occupations are higher than those found in the "male" professions, where women earn 74 to 90 percent of men's salaries. That there is a wage gap at all in predominantly female professions, however, attests to asymmetries in the workplace experiences of male and female tokens. These salary figures indicate that the men who do "women's work" fare as well as, and often better than, the women who work in these fields.

Although men certainly contribute to their own professional standing through their personal effort (discussed in detail in chapter 6), they face organizational pressures in these occupations that affect their success, independent of their ambition and effort. This chapter

Table 4
*Median Weekly Earnings of
Full-Time Professional Workers, by Sex, and Ratio
of Female:Male Earnings, 1990*

Occupation	Both	Men	Women	Ratio
Registered Nurses	608	616	608	.99
Elementary Teachers	519	575	513	.89
Librarians	489	—[a]	479	—
Social Workers	445	483	427	.88
Engineers	814	822	736	.90
Physicians	892	978	802	.82
College Teachers	747	808	620	.77
Lawyers	1,045	1,178	875	.74

SOURCE: U.S. Department of Labor, Bureau of Labor Statistics, *Employment and Earnings* 38, no. 1 (January 1991), table 56, p. 223.

[a]The Labor Department does not report income averages for base sample sizes consisting of fewer than 50,000 individuals.

investigates how opportunities are structured for men in these professions. In particular, I examine how hiring decisions, workplace culture, and interactions with clients affect men's careers. Men sometimes encounter prejudice, and even discrimination in these occupations. But unlike women in nontraditional occupations, the consequences of this prejudice actually can benefit men.

Hiring Decisions

Contrary to the experience of many women in the male-dominated professions, many of the men and women I spoke to indicated that there is a *preference* for hiring men in these four occupations. A Texas librarian at a junior high school said that his school district "would hire a male over a female":

[CW: Why do you think that is?]

Because there are so few, and the . . . ones that they do have, the library directors seem to really . . . think they're doing great jobs. I don't know, maybe they just feel they're being progressive or something, [but] I have had a real sense that they really appreciate having a male, particularly at the junior high. . . . As I said, when seven of us lost our jobs from the high schools and were redistributed, there were only four positions at junior high, and I got one of them. Three of the librarians, some who had been here longer than I had with the school district, were put down in elementary school as librarians. And I definitely think that being male made a difference in my being moved to the junior high rather than an elementary school.

Many of the men perceived their token status as males in predominantly female occupations as an *advantage* in hiring and promotions. When I asked an Arizona teacher whether his specialty (elementary special education) was an unusual area for men compared to other areas within education, he said,

Much more so. I am extremely marketable in special education. That's not why I got into the field. But I am extremely marketable because I am a man.

In several cases, the more female the specialty, the greater the apparent preference for men. For example, when asked if he encountered any problem getting a job in pediatrics, a Massachusetts nurse said,

No, no, none. . . . I've heard this from managers and supervisory-type people with men in pediatrics: "It's nice to have a man because it's such a female-dominated profession."

Hiring decisions are often based on supervisors' stereotypes of appropriate roles for men and women. Frequently these stereotypes benefit men, as was the case with one Massachusetts librarian. He was one of only two men in his first paraprofessional library job, which sparked controversy among the agency's higher administration:

> I found out after I'd been hired, that there were serious questions raised about . . . what my then supervisor—a woman librarian—had done because she was hiring two men essentially for clerical duties and that just went against the grain of everything that the people had seen before. They were used to men supervising the women in clerical jobs. But the idea of having a woman, and then sitting two men down in the secretarial pool under her supervision really made it difficult.

His supervisor's boss intervened and promoted him to a supervisory position—before he completed his professional training. He explained,

> He [the supervisor's boss] tended to move people not on the basis of their credentials so much as on the kind of skills and interests and impetus that they showed, and his own feelings about what they were capable of doing.

He believed that he was promoted to his first professional position to satisfy the administration's sense of "appropriate" jobs for men and women.

Sometimes the preference for men in these occupations is institutionalized. One man landed his first job in teaching before he earned the appropriate credential "because I was a wrestler and they wanted a wrestling coach." A female math teacher similarly told of her inability to find a full-time teaching position because the schools she applied to reserved the math jobs for people (presumably men) who could double as coaches.

In some cases, however, supervisors' gender stereotypes worked against men. For example, a social worker told me his boss preferred to hire women because he believed they were more tractable employees:

> Almost all of his appointments are women. I think that he simply finds women more collaborative, more willing to take orders. The men who report to him, almost all of whom he has inherited, are much more likely to challenge his position. So just about all of his appointments have been women.

In some cases, formal policies actually barred men from certain jobs. Such was the case in some rural Texas school districts, which refused to hire men in the youngest grades (K–3). Some male nurses also reported being excluded from positions in obstetrics and gynecology wards, a policy encountered more frequently in private Catholic hospitals. A particularly egregious example of policies based on stereotyping occurred in a large metropolitan public library system. Most of the men in the library system worked in the city's main library, as opposed to the neighborhood branches. According to a librarian who worked there, this was because one administrator had definite stereotypes about where men were most needed:

> We didn't have security guards [in the main library building]. Since this administrator worked in this building, and she could move people from the

branches, she decided she wanted to have men in the main library to sort of double as security guards. . . .

[CW: Do you resent that?]

Well, I don't want to work in the branches, so it's fine with me. But certainly, that's been true of other men. There was a guy that worked in the finest neighborhood branch. And they called him up and said, "Next week show up in Main, you've been transferred." And he certainly objected, and he's never been happy ever since.

Often the pressures keeping men out of certain specialties were more subtle than this. Some men described being "tracked" into practice areas within their professions which were considered more legitimate for men. For example, one Texas man described how he was pushed into administration and planning in social work, even though "I'm not interested in writing policy; I'm much more interested in research and clinical stuff." A nurse who is interested in pursuing graduate study in family and child health in Boston said he was dissuaded from entering the program specialty in favor of a concentration in "adult nursing." And a kindergarten teacher described his difficulty finding a job in his specialty after graduation: "I was recruited immediately to start getting into a track to become an administrator. And it was men who recruited me. It was men that ran the system at that time, especially in Los Angeles."

This tracking may bar men from the most female-identified specialties within these professions. But men are effectively being "kicked upstairs" in the process. Those specialties considered more legitimate practice areas for men also tend to be the most prestigious, and better-paying specialties as well. For example, men in nursing are overrepresented in critical care and psychiatric specialties, which tend to be higher paying than the others.[2] The highest paying and most prestigious library types are the academic libraries (where men are 35 percent of librarians) and the special libraries which are typically associated with businesses or other private organizations (where men constitute 20 percent of librarians).[3]

A distinguished kindergarten teacher, who had been voted citywide "Teacher of the Year," described the informal pressures he faced to advance in his field. He told me that even though people were pleased to see him in the classroom, "there's been some encouragement to think about administration, and there's been some encouragement to think about teaching at the university level or something like that, or supervisory-type position."

The effect of this "tracking" is the opposite of that experienced by women in male-dominated occupations. Researchers have reported that many women encounter "glass ceilings" in their efforts to scale organizational and professional hierarchies. That is, they reach invisible barriers to promotion in their careers, caused mainly by the sexist attitudes of men in the highest positions.[4] In contrast to this "glass ceiling," many of the men I interviewed seem to encounter a "glass escalator." Often, despite their intentions, they face invisible pressures to move up in their professions. Like being on a moving escalator, they have to work to stay in place.

A public librarian specializing in children's collections (a heavily female concentration) described an encounter with this "escalator" in his very first job out of library school. In his first six-months' evaluation, his supervisors commended him for his good work in storytelling and related activities, but they criticized him for "not shooting high enough":

> Seriously. That's literally what they were telling me. They assumed that because I was a male—and they told me this—and that I was being hired right out of graduate school, that somehow I wasn't doing the kind of management-oriented work that they thought I should be doing. And as a result, really they had a lot of bad marks, as it were, against me on my evaluation. And I said I couldn't believe this!

Throughout his ten-year career, he has had to struggle to remain in the children's collections.

The "glass escalator" does not operate at all levels. In particular, men in academia reported some gender-based discrimination in the highest positions due to their universities' commitment to affirmative action. Two nursing professors reported that they felt their own chances of promotion to deanships were nil because their universities viewed the position of dean of nursing as a guaranteed female appointment in an otherwise heavily male-dominated administrative capacity. One social work professor reported that his university had canceled his school's search for a dean because no minority candidates, male or female, had been placed on their short list. The rumor was that the other schools on campus were permitted to go forward with their searches—even though they also failed to put forward names of minority candidates—because the higher administration perceived it to be "easier" to fulfill affirmative action goals in the social work school. There appeared to be more evidence of the "glass escalator" at work in the lower levels of the predominantly female professions.

Of course, men's motivations also play a role in their advancement to higher professional positions. I do not mean to suggest that the men I interviewed all resented or resisted the informal tracking they experienced. As noted in chapter 3, some men entered these occupations anticipating that they would ride the "glass escalator": They planned to move into administration or management as quickly as possible. Furthermore, personal ambition also plays a role in accounting for men's movement into more "male-defined" arenas within these professions (see chapter 6). But these occupations structure opportunities for males independent of their individual desires or motives. That is, men face pressures to succeed in spite of their own ambition.

The interviews suggest that men often receive preferential treatment in hiring and promotions because of their gender. Although some cases of gender discrimination in the hiring process were mentioned, this often resulted in the men being channeled into more "masculine" specialties within these professions, which ironically meant being "tracked" into better paying and more prestigious specialties.

Supervisors and Colleagues: The Working Environment

Researchers claim that subtle forms of workplace discrimination push women out of male-dominated occupations.[5] In particular, women report feeling excluded from informal leadership and decision-making networks, and they sense hostility from their male co-workers, which makes them feel uncomfortable and unwanted.[6] Respondents in this study were asked about their relationships with supervisors and female colleagues to ascertain whether men also experienced "poisoned" work environments when entering nontraditional occupations.

A major difference in the experience of men and women in nontraditional occupations is that men are far more likely to be supervised by a member of their own sex. In each of the four professions I studied, men are overrepresented in administrative and managerial capacities, or, as in the case of nursing, the organizational hierarchy is governed by men. For example, 15 percent of all elementary school teachers are men, but men make up over 80 percent of all elementary school principals and 96 percent of all public school superintendents and assistant superintendents.[7] Likewise, over 40 percent of all male social workers hold administrative or managerial positions, compared to 30 percent of all female social workers.[8] And 50 percent of male librarians hold administrative positions, compared to 30 percent of female librarians, and the majority of deans and directors of major university and public libraries are men.[9] Thus, unlike women who enter "male fields," the men in these professions often work under the direct supervision of other men.

Many of the men interviewed reported that they had good rapport with their male supervisors. It was not uncommon in education, for example, for the male principal to informally socialize with the male staff, as a Texas special education teacher describes:

> Occasionally I've had a principal who would regard me as "the other man on the campus" and "it's us against them," you know? I mean, nothing really that extreme, except that some male principals feel like there's nobody there to talk to except the other man. So I've been in that position.

These personal ties can have important consequences for men's careers. For example, one California nurse, whose performance was judged marginal by his nursing superiors, was transferred to the emergency room staff (a prestigious promotion) due to his personal friendship with the physician in charge. And a Massachusetts teacher acknowledged that his principal's personal interest in him landed him his current job:

> [CW: You had mentioned that your principal had sort of spotted you at your previous job and had wanted to bring you here [to this school]. Do you think that has anything to do with the fact that you're a man, aside from your skills as a teacher?]
>
> Yes, I would say in that particular case, that was part of it. . . . We have certain things in common, certain interests that really lined up.
>
> [CW: Vis-à-vis teaching?]
>
> Well, more extraneous things—running specifically, and music. And we just seemed to get along real well right off the bat. It is just kind of a guy thing; we just liked each other. . . .

Interviewees did not report many instances of male supervisors discriminating against them, or refusing to accept them because they were male. Indeed, these men were much more likely to report that their male bosses discriminated against the *females* in their professions. When asked if he thought physicians treated male and female nurses differently, a Texas nurse said:

> I think yeah, some of them do. I think the women seem like they have a lot more trouble with the physicians treating them in a derogatory manner. Or, if not derogatory, then in a very paternalistic way than

the men [are treated]. Usually if a physician is mad at a male nurse, he just kind of yells at him. Kind of like an employee. And if they're mad at a female nurse, rather than treat them on an equal basis, in terms of just letting their anger out at them as an employee, they're more paternalistic or there's some sexual harassment component to it.

A Texas teacher perceived a similar situation where he worked:

I've never felt unjustly treated by a principal because I'm a male. The principals that I've seen that I felt are doing things that are kind of arbitrary or not well thought out are doing it to everybody. In fact, they're probably doing it to the females worse than they are to me.

However, one nurse did tell me about an exception to this generally favorable treatment. During the fire drills at a Catholic hospital where he worked (which was administered by men), the male nurses were required "to report to the site of the fire with the maintenance department and housekeeping," while the female nurses were required to "stay on the floor and close the doors and make sure that everything is out of the hall." The administrators assumed that the men, and not the women, could help combat fires—a distinction that hardly favored the men.

There are also indications that supervisors treat openly gay men less favorably than straight men. For example, a nurse in Texas told me that one of the physicians he worked with would prefer to staff the operating room with male nurses exclusively—as long as they were not gay. And a Massachusetts social worker told me that he was passed over for promotion because he did not seem masculine enough:

> They were going to hire a social worker and I sort of thought for sure I would get that job, but in fact I did not get that job. They wanted somebody more assertive, more aggressive. . . . I am someone who is pretty even-keeled, soft-spoken, and often that gets interpreted, particularly by men, as being ineffectual, and that is what happened there. . . . It was a group of men who were interviewing me and they felt that I couldn't, sort of, be more male-like. . . . I mean, they didn't say it, but that's my interpretation of it.

Thus, although in general, respondents believed that male supervisors treated men more favorably than they treated women, there were some notable exceptions to this rule.

Of course, not all the men who work in these occupations are supervised by men. Many of the men interviewed who had female bosses also reported high levels of acceptance—although the level of intimacy they achieved with women did not seem as great as with other men. But in some cases, men reported feeling shut-out from decision making when the higher administration was constituted entirely by women. I asked this Arizona librarian whether men in the library profession were discriminated against in hiring because of their sex:

> Professionally speaking, people go to considerable lengths to keep that kind of thing out of their [hiring] deliberations. Personally, is another matter. It's pretty common around here to talk about the "old girl network." This is one of the few libraries that I've had any intimate knowledge of which is actually

controlled by women. . . . Most of the department heads and upper level administrators are women. And there's an "old girl network" that works just like the "old boy network," except that the important conferences take place in the women's room rather than on the golf course. But the political mechanism is the same, the exclusion of the other sex from decision making is the same. The reasons are the same. It's somewhat discouraging. . . .

Although I did not interview many supervisors, I did include twenty-three women in my sample to ascertain their perspectives about the presence of men in their professions. All of the women I interviewed claimed to be supportive of their male colleagues, but some conveyed ambivalence. For example, a social work professor said she would like to see more men enter the social work profession, particularly in the clinical specialty (where they are underrepresented). She said she would favor affirmative action hiring guidelines for men in the profession, and yet, she resented the fact that her department hired "another white male" during a recent search. I confronted her about this apparent ambivalence:

[CW: I find it very interesting that, on the one hand, you sort of perceive this preference and perhaps even sexism with regard to how men are evaluated and how they achieve higher positions within the profession, yet, on the other hand, you would be encouraging of more men to enter the field. Is that contradictory to you, or . . . ?]

Yeah, it's contradictory.

A similar feeling was related to me by another social worker. After she described the meteoric rise of a young man in the agency where she works, I asked whether she thought the women workers facilitated men's advancement in any way. She said,

> Absolutely. I think the women expect the men to come in and pass them by. These are older women. They expect the young white male to exceed them, and they give them a hand up. I don't hear any anger. I hear them slapping them on the back: "Go on, Charlie! You're twenty-nine; isn't that cute? I'm fifty-nine; my son is your age. Charlie's going to make it to the top."

> [CW: Do you think that's different from the younger women that you see?]

> I think maybe we're a little more skeptical, angry, and resentful. And we're more apt to try to be peers with these guys. But you can see how it sets up for some anger. We all have the same student loans. Women actually have more work at home.

Men's reception by their female colleagues is thus somewhat mixed. It appears that women are generally eager to see men enter "their" occupations, and the women I interviewed claimed they were supportive of their male peers. Indeed, several men agreed with this social worker that their female colleagues had facilitated their careers in various ways (including college mentorship). At the same time, however, women often resent the apparent ease with which men seem to advance within these professions, sensing that men at the higher levels receive preferential treatment, and thus close off advancement opportunities for women.

But this ambivalence does not seem to translate into the "poisoned" work environment described by many women who work in male-dominated occupations. Among the male interviewees, there were no accounts of sexual harassment (indeed, one man claimed this was a disappointment to him!). However, women do treat their male colleagues differently on occasion. It is not uncommon in nursing, for example, for men to be called upon to help catheterize male patients, or to lift especially heavy patients. Some librarians also said that women asked them to lift and move heavy boxes of books because they were men. And male teachers occasionally confront differential treatment as well, as described by this Texas teacher:

> As a man, you're teaching with all women, and that can be hard sometimes. Just because of the stereotypes, you know. I'm real into computers . . . , and all the time people are calling me to fix their computer. Or if somebody gets a flat tire, they come and get me. I mean, there are just a lot of stereotypes. Not that I mind doing any of those things, but it's . . . you know, it just kind of bugs me that it is a stereotype—"A man should do that." Or if their kids have a lot of discipline problems, that kiddo's in your room. Or if there are kids that don't have a father in their home, that kid's in your room. Hell, nowadays that'd be half the school in my room. [laughs] But you know, all the time I hear from the principal or from other teachers, "Well, this child really needs a man . . . a male role model." [laughs] So there are a lot of stereotypes that . . . men kind of get stuck with.

Another stereotype confronting men, in nursing and social work in particular, is the expectation that they are better able than women to handle aggressive individuals and diffuse violent situations. An Arizona social worker who was the first male caseworker in a rural district, described this preference for men:

They welcomed a man, particularly in child welfare. Sometimes you have to go into some tough parts of towns and cities, and they felt it was nice to have a man around to accompany them or be present when they were dealing with a difficult client. Or just doing things that males can do. I always felt very welcomed.

But this special treatment bothered some respondents: Getting assigned all the violent patients or discipline problems can make for difficult and unpleasant working conditions. Nurses, for example, described how they were called upon to subdue violent patients. A traveling psychiatric nurse I interviewed in Texas told how his female colleagues gave him "plenty of opportunities" to use his wrestling skills:

The females will go in and stir up the patient, and then expect you to go in and either calm him down or tie him down. "Well, we just went in and raised real issues with this man." And I say, "What are you doing that for? Who wants to be ticked off?" "Well, we wanted to get him to express his anger." They get him to express it, but then you're the one who's got to deal with it. They're being real therapeutic, but when push comes to shove, they want no part of it. They stand in the background while—we used a lot of restraints in L.A. and Philadelphia.

But many men claimed that this differential treatment did not distress them. In fact, several said they liked being appreciated for the special traits and abilities (such as strength) they could contribute to their professions.

Furthermore, women's special treatment of men sometimes enhanced—rather than detracted from—the men's work environments. One Texas librarian said he felt

"more comfortable working with women than men" because "I think it has something to do with control. Maybe
it's that women will let me take control more than men
will." Several men reported that their female colleagues
often cast them into leadership roles. For example, this
special education teacher who "team teaches" with a female, told me,

> We have an inside joke in our room because we have
> a lot of problems that we have to take care of,
> whether it's budget problems or whatever. She [the
> other teacher] says, "Jerry, we have a problem, and
> I need you to do your male bonding [with the prin-
> cipal]." [laughs] Jokingly. But then again, not so
> jokingly.
>
> [CW: Because she thinks maybe you can get further
> with him than . . . ?]
>
> And if it's true or not, we don't know, but we joke
> about it. And underneath it all, it may not be as big
> a joke as we think. Whether it's because I can come
> in and talk basketball and small talk, you know what
> I mean? Over my partner who is not able to do that
> because she doesn't feel comfortable. . . . It sounds
> awful! [laughs]. . . . I think it's that way because I feel
> more comfortable approaching him. I think I can go
> in and say, "Hey, Stan, I need some help, this is a
> screwy situation."

Not all of the men I interviewed liked being cast into leadership roles, but it did enhance their authority and control in the workplace.[10] In subtle (and not-so-subtle) ways,
then, this differential treatment contributed to the "glass
escalator" confronting these men in nontraditional professions.

Even outside of work, most of the men interviewed said

they felt fully accepted by their female colleagues. They were usually included in informal social occasions with the women—even though this sometimes meant attending baby showers or Tupperware parties. Many of the men said that they declined offers to attend these events because they were not interested in "women's things," although several others claimed to attend everything. The minority men I interviewed seemed to feel the least comfortable in these informal contexts. One social worker in Arizona was asked about socializing with his female colleagues:

> [CW: For example, if all the employees were going to get together to have a party, or celebrate a bridal shower or whatever, would you be invited along with the rest of the group?]

> They would invite me, I would say, somewhat reluctantly. Being a black male, working with all white females, it did cause some outside problems. So I didn't go to a lot of functions with them. . . .

> [CW: You felt that there was some tension there on the level of your acceptance?]

> Yeah. It was OK working, but on the outside, personally, there was some tension there. It never came out, that they said, "Because of who you are we can't invite you" [laughs], and I wouldn't have done anything anyway. I would have probably respected them more for saying what was on their minds. But I never felt completely in with the group.

Some single men also said they felt uncomfortable socializing with their married female colleagues because it gave the "wrong impression." But in general, the men said that they felt very comfortable around their colleagues, and they described their workplaces as very congenial for men.

The interviews suggest that the working environment encountered by "nontraditional" male workers is quite unlike that faced by women who work in traditionally male fields. Because it is not uncommon for men in predominantly female professions to be supervised by other men, they tend to have closer rapport and more intimate social relationships with people in management. These ties can facilitate men's careers by smoothing the way for future promotions. Relationships with female supervisors were also described for the most part in positive terms, although in some cases, men perceived an "old girls' " network in place that excluded them from decision making. But in sharp contrast to the reports of women in nontraditional occupations, men in these fields did not complain of feeling discriminated against because they were men. If anything, they felt that being male was an asset that enhanced their career prospects.

Those men interviewed for this study also described congenial workplaces, and a very high level of acceptance from their female colleagues. The sentiment was echoed by women I spoke to who said that they were pleased to see more men enter "their" professions. Some women, however, did express resentment over the "fast-tracking" that their male colleagues seem to experience. But this ambivalence did not translate into a hostile work environment for men: Women generally included men in their informal social events and, in some ways, even facilitated men's careers. By casting men into leadership roles, presuming they were more knowledgeable and qualified, or relying on them to perform certain critical tasks, women unwittingly contributed to the "glass escalator effect" facing men who do "women's work."

Relationships with Clients

Workers in these service-oriented occupations come into frequent contact with the public during the course of their work day. Nurses treat patients; social workers usually have client case loads; librarians serve patrons; and teachers are in constant contact with children, and often with parents as well. Many of those interviewed claimed that the clients they served had different expectations of men and women in these occupations, and often treated them differently.

People react with surprise and often disbelief when they encounter a man in nursing, elementary school teaching, and, to a lesser extent, librarianship. (Usually people have no clear expectations about the sex of social workers.) The stereotypes men face are often negative. For example, according to this Massachusetts nurse, it is frequently assumed that male nurses are gay:

> Fortunately, I carry one thing with me that protects me from [the stereotype that male nurses are gay], and the one thing I carry with me is a wedding ring, and it makes a big difference. The perfect example was conversations before I was married. . . .[People would ask], "Oh, do you have a girlfriend?" Or you'd hear patients asking questions along that idea, and they were simply implying, "Why is this guy in nursing? Is it because he's gay and he's a pervert?" And I'm not associating the two by any means, but this is the thought process.

Male teachers and librarians also encounter suspicions that they are gay. One kindergarten teacher told me about an early experience in his career, related to him years after the fact by his principal:

He indicated to me that parents had . . . a problem with the fact that I was a male. . . . I recall almost exactly what he said. There were three specific concerns that the parents had: One parent said, "How can he love my child; he's a man." The second thing that I recall, he said the parent said, "He has a beard." And the third thing was, "Aren't you concerned about homosexuality?"

It is not uncommon for both gay and straight men in these occupations to encounter people who believe that they are "gay 'til proven otherwise," as one nurse put it. In fact, there are many gay men employed in these occupations. But gender stereotypes are at least as responsible for this general belief as any "empirical" assessment of men's sexual lifestyles. To the degree that men in these professions are perceived as not "measuring up" to the supposedly more challenging occupational roles and standards demanded of "real" men, they are immediately suspected of being effeminate—"like women"—and thus, homosexual.

An equally prevalent sexual stereotype about men in these occupations is that they are potentially dangerous and abusive. Several men described special rules they followed to guard against the widespread presumption of sexual abuse. For example, nurses were sometimes required to have a female "chaperone" present when performing certain procedures or working with specific populations. This psychiatric nurse described a former workplace:

I worked on a floor for the criminally insane. Pretty threatening work. So you have to have a certain number of females on the floor just to balance out. Because there were female patients on the floor too.

And you didn't want to be accused of rape or any sex crimes.

Teachers and librarians described the steps they took to protect themselves from suspicions of sexual impropriety. A kindergarten teacher said:

> I know that I'm careful about how I respond to students. I'm careful in a number of ways—in my physical interaction with students. It's mainly to reassure parents. . . . For example, a little girl was very affectionate, very anxious to give me a hug. She'll just throw herself at me. I need to tell her very carefully: "Sonia, you need to tell me when you want to hug me." That way I can come down, crouch down. Because you don't want a child giving you a hug on your hip. You just don't want to do that. So I'm very careful about body position.

And this probation officer described how his department dealt with sexual harassment charges raised against him:

> I transported one of my women probationers to the county jail in handcuffs. . . . When I left her in the county jail, she was telling the other women on the cell block that I had molested her on the way to [the jail]. And so, when the story came out, my department transferred the first woman [probation officer] from juvenile probation to adult probation to assign to women's cases.

These popular prejudices can be damaging to self-esteem and they probably push some men out of these professions altogether (see chapter 6). Yet, ironically, these stereotypes sometimes contribute to the "glass escalator effect" I have been describing. Men seem to encounter the most vituperative criticism from the public when they are in the most feminine-identified specialties. Concerns voiced by the public sometimes result in men being shunted into more "legitimate" positions for men. This is what happened to one librarian in charge of the children's collections at a branch library, who now works in the reference department of the city's main library:

> Some of the people [who frequented the branch library] complained that they didn't want to have a man doing the storytelling scenario. And I got transferred here to the central library in an equivalent job. . . . I thought that I did a good job. And I had been told by my supervisor that I was doing a good job.

> [CW: Have you ever considered filing some sort of lawsuit to get that other job back?]

> Well, actually, the job I've gotten now . . . well, it's [as] a reference librarian; it's what I wanted in the first place. I've got a whole lot more authority here. I'm also in charge of the circulation desk. And I've recently been promoted because of my new stature, so . . . no, I'm not considering trying to get that other job back.

Although negative stereotypes about men who do "women's work" can push men out of specific jobs, their effects can actually benefit men. Instead of being a source of negative discrimination, these prejudices can add to the "glass escalator effect" by pressuring men to move *out* of the most feminine-identified areas and *up* to those regarded as more legitimate for men.

The public's reactions to men working in these occupations, however, are by no means always negative. Several men and women reported that people often assume that men in these occupations are more competent than women, or that they bring special skills and expertise to their professional practice. For example, a female academic librarian told me that patrons usually address their questions to the male reference librarian when there is a choice between asking a male or a female. A male clinical social worker in private practice claimed that both men and women generally preferred male psychotherapists. And several male nurses told me that people often assume that they are physicians and direct their medical inquires to them instead of to the female nurses.[11]

The presumption that men are more competent than women is another difference in the experience of token men and women. Women who work in nontraditional occupations are often suspected of being incompetent, unable to survive the pressures of "men's work." As a consequence, these women often report feeling compelled to prove themselves and, as the saying goes, "work twice as hard as men to be considered half as good." To the degree that men are assumed to be competent and in control, they may have to be twice as incompetent to be considered half as bad. One man claimed that "if you're a mediocre male teacher, you're considered a better teacher than if you're a female and a mediocre teacher. I think there's that prejudice there." Qualities considered assets in a man become debits in a woman, according to this Massachusetts nurse:

> Men are supposed to be out there, be the breadwinner, be confrontive and do all those types of things. And I know a lot of women that are like that, but they're called bitches. And I'm not. . . . I have a "strong personality"; they're a "bitch." Which is unfortunate.

There are different standards and assumptions about men's competence that follow them into nontraditional occupations. In contrast, women in both traditional and nontraditional occupations must contend with the presumption that they are neither competent nor qualified.

Clients sometimes articulate specific reasons for preferring men over women. Male teachers and school librarians frequently encounter the stereotype that they are better than women at disciplining children. A special education teacher, for example, explained why parents preferred placing their children in his room:

> In special education, there are more boy than girl students. And many of these students have hyperactivity or behavior problems. The parents who are aware that their child is having behavior problems in school feel comfortable when they know that child is going to a man because they believe a man will control the behavior more than a female teacher [will].

Not everyone interviewed agreed that men were actually better than women at establishing rapport with boys. But almost all had encountered this expectation.

Men in social work and nursing are also expected to have better ability than women to relate to men and men's special needs. Men sometimes request a male caseworker because, according to one social worker, some men "just feel uncomfortable opening up to a female and talking about personal things." Male nurses are sometimes preferred to perform certain intimate procedures on male patients, such as catheterizations. As one male nurse put it, "sometimes males get embarrassed by female nurses."

The reasons that clients give for preferring or rejecting men reflect the complexity of our society's stereotypes about masculinity and femininity. Masculinity is often associated with competence and mastery, in contrast to femininity, which is often associated with instrumental incompetence. Because of these stereotypes, men are perceived as being stricter disciplinarians and stronger than women, and thus better able to handle violent or potentially violent situations.

But these positive masculine stereotypes are probably linked to the general fear that men in these professions are sexual perverts who will exploit their intimate access to vulnerable populations (children, clients, patients) for sexual gain. This may be the flipside of the stereotype of masculine competence and control: Masculinity shades into domination, into sexual domination in particular. On the other hand, we saw that men who either fail to conform or refuse to conform to masculine stereotypes are immediately suspected of homosexuality.

These beliefs about male sexuality form a kind of double bind for men in these professions. If men appear to conform to the stereotypes of masculinity (mastery and control), they are open to suspicions of being sexually abusive or exploitative. If they do not "measure up" to masculine expectations, they are suspected of being homosexual. In other words, men in these occupations face prejudice if they are considered *too* masculine and if they are considered not masculine *enough*. One female teacher articulated this double bind quite well when asked if she would like to see more men enter the teaching profession. She said yes, as long as they did not fit either the "sissy" stereotype or the "macho" stereotype. As we will see in chapter 6, navigating between these two extremes presents quite a challenge to the men in these professions.

Conclusion

Both men and women who work in nontraditional occupations encounter discrimination, but the forms and the consequences of this discrimination are very different for the two groups. Unlike "nontraditional" women workers, most of the discrimination and prejudice facing men in the "female" professions comes from clients. For the most part, the men and women I interviewed believed that men are given fair—if not preferential—treatment in hiring and promotion decisions, are accepted by their supervisors and colleagues, and are well-integrated into the workplace subculture. Indeed, there seem to be subtle mechanisms in place that enhance men's positions in these professions—a phenomenon I refer to as a "glass escalator effect."

Men encounter their most "mixed" reception in their dealings with clients, who often react negatively to male nurses, teachers, and to a lesser extent, librarians. Many people assume that the men are sexually suspect if they are employed in these "feminine" occupations either because they do or they do not conform to stereotypical masculine characteristics.

Dealing with the stress of these negative stereotypes can be overwhelming, and it probably pushes some men out of these occupations.[12] The challenge facing the men who stay in these fields is to accentuate their positive contribution to what our society defines as essentially "women's work." In chapter 6 I examine men's efforts to negotiate their masculine identity amidst these conflicting stereotypes and assumptions.

6

Masculinity in "Feminine" Occupations

Masculinity is an extremely elusive concept (as is femininity for that matter). A new subdiscipline called "men's studies" is fast developing in academia, dedicated to analyzing this peculiar feature of men's identity. Meanwhile, a popular "men's movement" offers seminars, literature, and "wildman" retreats to help men get in touch with their masculinity. But despite this outpouring of interest—perhaps even because of it—masculinity has become an increasingly confusing and obscure notion.

This chapter reviews theories of masculinity, and then explores what it means to the men in nursing, elementary school teaching, librarianship, and social work to be masculine. As we have seen, these men are often confronted with the charge that they are *not* masculine because of the kind of work they do. Reflecting on the reasons for men's underrepresentation in elementary education, a kindergarten teacher said,

> It's just not a traditional man's job, and I think a lot of men think of that. You know, when you go into

college, if you say you're in elementary ed, that's just not a real cool thing to be in. . . . It's definitely not a thing that you would do if you felt a need to have a macho image.

Paradoxically, however, many of the men I interviewed *did* feel "a need to have a macho image." But convincing themselves and others that they are appropriately masculine is not a simple task. Granted the negative stereotypes about them and their occupations, they must actively constitute and manage their identity as men. This chapter explores the various strategies men use to assert and maintain their masculinity.

Precisely because their masculinity is challenged, these men may be more aware than other men of the steps they take to sustain their masculinity, making them an excellent case study to explore the general dynamics of "doing gender."[1] This is a term coined by sociologists Candace West and Don Zimmerman to describe how beliefs about gender differences are created and sustained in daily, ritualized interactions. By engaging in certain behaviors, and assiduously avoiding others, men in these occupations can convey to their supervisors, clients, and coworkers that they are unlike their female peers, thereby preserving a sense of themselves as masculine. Exactly how these men "do gender" is perhaps more obvious and apparent than how men "do gender" in contexts where masculinity is not contested. In a sense they represent exaggerated cases of gender performance—analytically very similar to transsexuals who feel they must constantly prove to others their "true" gender identity. But, as David Morgan argues, precisely because they are "anomalies," the experiences of these men in nontraditional occupations "can be treated as mini-dramas through which we can begin to explore the tensions and complexities of gender identities and the gender order."[2]

Thus the focus of this chapter is *how* men in "feminine" occupations reproduce their masculinity. But before beginning this discussion, we must first settle on a definition of masculinity.

The Meaning of Masculinity

The concept of gender as a socially constructed identity is of relatively recent historical origin. While the terms "masculinity" and "femininity" have been in usage for centuries, they generally signified biological characteristics or traits (when applied to people). Being born a man or a woman was believed to have inevitable consequences for how people thought, felt, and behaved. In the more modern formulation, popular only since the 1970s, gender is perceived as socially and culturally mediated and variable: It is the social meaning given to biological differences, internalized by individuals, that constitutes gender identity.[3]

But aside from agreeing that gender is a social construction, and not a biological necessity, there is very little consensus among social scientists about what it means to be masculine or feminine. If biological markers should no longer be used, how do we know that someone is masculine? What does it mean to have a masculine identity?

One of the early efforts to define masculinity focused on the traits or personality characteristics of individuals. Psychologists catalogued traits as "masculine," "feminine," or "neutral," and then asked individuals to gauge how well they matched each trait. Everyone selecting a majority of the masculine traits was defined as masculine. Using these methods, researchers "discovered" that some women have "masculine" personalities, and some men have "feminine" personalities, thus demonstrating the difference between masculinity and anatomical maleness.

This kind of personality testing has been used repeatedly to assess whether men in predominantly female occupations are more "feminine" than "regular" men.[4] A recent example is a study by Michael Galbraith, who administered the Bem Sex Role Inventory (BSRI), one of the most popular of the masculinity-femininity scales, to male nurses, elementary school teachers, and engineers to discern which group was more "masculine." The BSRI "measures" masculinity and femininity by asking respondents on a seven-point scale how closely they conform to thirty personality traits, such as "aggressive" (a masculine trait), "yielding" (a feminine trait), and "friendly" (a neutral trait). "Masculine" individuals score high on only the masculine traits (those who score high on both masculine and feminine traits are labeled "androgynous"). Galbraith found that a higher percentage of the engineers scored in the pure masculine range—30.9 percent (versus 23.4 percent of the nurses and 16.7 percent of the teachers). The highest percentage of teachers and nurses were categorized "androgynous," meaning that they scored high on *both* masculine and feminine traits. However, Galbraith pointed out that the nurses and teachers had higher average masculinity scores than the engineers. He concluded that "men in nontraditional work retain traditional components of their masculinity."[5]

This research is useful for discrediting the most egregious stereotypes about men who work in female occupations. Galbraith's study challenges the widespread belief that these men are "anomalies" by showing that male nurses and teachers are really not that different from male engineers. But several questions are not addressed by this type of research. Most importantly, it does not question why certain attributes are considered masculine, or how and why these stereotypes develop. In fact, this research tends to reify the very gendered categories it seeks to undermine, a problem that Sandra Bem, the inventor of the BSRI, now acknowledges:

> In the early 1970s, I focused almost exclusively on the concept of androgyny (from the Greek terms an-dro, meaning male, and gyne, meaning female) because that concept seemed to challenge the traditional categories of masculine and feminine as nothing before had ever done. By the late 1970s and early 1980s, however, I had begun to see that the concept of androgyny inevitably focuses so much more attention on the individual's being both masculine and feminine than on the culture's having created the concepts of masculinity and femininity in the first place that it can legitimately be said to reproduce precisely the gender polarization that it seeks to undercut.[6]

Research using the masculinity-femininity scales confirms that few people measure up to gender stereotypes—which is an important finding—but it does not tell us very much about the reproduction of masculinity in society, or the meaning of masculinity in men's lives.[7]

A second approach that has been used to define masculinity (and femininity) focuses on roles, or patterned sets of behaviors. This approach, which has been the dominant one among U.S. sociologists since the 1950s, maintains that men are socialized to be masculine by their work and family roles. According to sex role theory, men take on characteristics required of them by their jobs and by their role as father in the family; they are molded by society to conform to expectations embedded in these positions. Men are instrumental, logical, nonemotional, disciplinarians—personality traits required of them to fulfill their roles in society.[8]

Sex role theory is very compelling to sociologists because it emphasizes that society (not the individual) produces masculinity. Individuals are conceived as "tabula rasa," ready to be molded by the demands of the social structure. To change an individual's disposition, one simply has to change the individual's social role.

This perspective could be applied to men's experiences in female occupations. As I argue in chapter 5, many of the men employed in these occupations work in specialties where they are expected to demonstrate traditionally masculine characteristics—as administrators, technical specialists, and even disciplinarians of young children. Those men who attempt to reject these roles nevertheless face myriad pressures to conform, demonstrating that to some extent, men are shaped by their social settings.

But men also participate in the shaping of their roles; they are not entirely passive in the process of producing masculinity. Men in these occupations struggle (often in very creative ways) to carve out a niche for themselves they can label as "masculine." Why men might want to do this is left unexplained by traditional sex role theory.

There are other limitations to role theory besides ignoring individual agency. The theory does not explain why sex roles are divided (except to say that society requires it), nor does it account for the higher value placed on male roles. Cynthia Fuchs Epstein, a contemporary proponent of role theory, acknowledges these limitations. She maintains that gender role distinctions are invidious and "deceptive" and marshals considerable evidence to show that men's roles are more highly regarded than women's, yet she dismisses any attempt to explain the causes of gender differentiation and male privilege: "How does this happen?" she asks. "We shall never know."[9]

Other perspectives are better equipped than role theory to address these questions. In particular, I have found feminist psychoanalytic theory a useful framework for explaining both gender differentiation and female subordination. Psychoanalytic theory is a highly contested perspective in sociology for a variety of reasons, but combined with a feminist analysis of men's power and advantage in society, I believe it can illuminate the meaning of masculinity for men in female occupations.

Psychoanalytic theorists never exactly specify the contents of masculinity, except to argue that males typically define masculinity negatively, as whatever is not feminine. This definition stems from the experience of being "mothered" as a child: Most children in western societies are reared almost exclusively by women (usually their mothers), especially during the earliest years of life, resulting in a "feminine identification." This means that the child first develops a sense of his or her selfhood in a close, one-on-one relationship with the mother, and qualities possessed by the mother are internalized by the infant to form the beginnings of the child's personality. If adult women exhibit emotional expressiveness and nurturance in their relationships with their newborns, these qualities will form the core of the infant's identity.[10]

Males and females follow similar patterns of identity and personality formation until around age three. At that age, boys are typically encouraged (often by their fathers) to replace their identification with their mothers in favor of a "masculine" identification. This is usually a traumatic experience for the boy because, essentially, he is required to "give up" the attachment that means the most to him, and he is threatened (usually by the father) if he refuses. Furthermore, achieving a masculine identity is problematic since adult men are typically absent during most of the young child's waking hours. They are simply not as available as mothers (and other adult women) for the kind of intimate bonding and interaction that produces in boys their original feminine identification. The only positive associations with masculinity sons typically learn from their "absent" fathers are work and heterosexuality—reflecting the traditional role of fathers in nuclear families. But these roles are very abstract to most children; their relationships with their fathers (or other adult men, for that matter) lack the concreteness and intimacy of their relationships with their mothers (and adult women in general). Boys therefore come to define masculinity negatively, as whatever is not feminine. They will often invent "masculinity rituals" to fill out the shape and contents of their new identities, typically condemning anything associated with femininity as inferior in the process. Psychoanalytic theorists view this disparagement of femininity as a kind of compensation for the boys' loss of their original, fulfilling attachment to and identification with their mothers.[11]

The greater power of the father forms another incentive for the boy's separation from his mother and disparagement of femininity. This power is both real and symbolic: real because men often control the economic resources and major decision making that goes on in the family; and symbolic insofar as the father represents the "phallus," the privileged position in language and other forms of cultural discourse.[12] Thus the boy is encouraged to renounce his feminine identification in order to share in the power and the superior cultural value attached to the "phallus." Therefore, to be masculine to him usually means to be *different from* and *better than* women. Men raised in a traditional nuclear family setting typically (although by no means always) unconsciously strive to achieve this gender differentiation.[13]

Psychoanalytic theory, especially in its feminist versions, provides a far superior definition of masculinity than the major alternative approaches in sociology. This perspective stresses that gender is a process of differentiation, not two static and inflexible sets of character traits or social roles. According to psychoanalytic theory, the content of masculinity is not given; it is constantly shifting and changing because it is always defined in opposition to women and femininity (which itself is a fluid concept). Furthermore, psychoanalytic theory is better equipped than the alternatives to explain variation in the subjective experience of masculinity. The theory explicitly recognizes that not all men will experience the same needs and desires to differentiate themselves from women. Group differences in the definition of masculinity are even likely: For example, those raised in families where men participate in child rearing will probably not define masculinity as the opposite of nurturing and emotional expressiveness.[14]

Moreover, psychoanalytic theory recognizes that becoming masculine or feminine usually entails conflict and ambivalence, unlike the alternative theories which tend to view men and women as acquiescent and untroubled by their gender socialization. Psychoanalytic theorists, following Freud, define masculinity as a psychic construction achieved at considerable and ongoing cost to the individual. Gender identity is never acquired in a straightforward way: Fantasy, projection, and repression distort experience and threaten to derail the process at any point. Indeed, childhood traumas are rarely ever resolved; for many men, masculinity is an ongoing struggle that is never completely "accomplished."

Finally, the definition of masculinity offered by psychoanalytic theory acknowledges that many men desire to dominate women. Trait theory and sex role theory either do not acknowledge or do not explain the antagonism toward women that is so prevalent in men. In contrast, Freud and other psychoanalytic theorists contend that masculinity "normally" entails a "triumphant contempt" for women.[15] As Lynne Segal has argued, this is one of the few theories that can explain "the intensities of men's paranoia over masculinity, their endemic violence towards women, and the cultural fear and hatred of women."[16]

But there are limitations to the psychoanalytic approach. The theory does not explain why men are able to force their psychological concerns on others. That is, the theory does not tell us why men's preoccupations with difference and subordination prevail in our culture, nor how they come to be embedded in our social institutions. Also missing from psychoanalytic theory is an explanation of why masculinity assumes particular historical forms. While it does help to explain variation in the subjective experience of gender identity, it does not account for the ascendence of specific configurations of masculinity and femininity in particular social contexts.[17]

To address these problems in psychoanalytic theory, R. W. Connell developed a concept he calls "hegemonic masculinity," the socially dominant form of masculinity in any given historical period. Qualities currently associated with hegemonic masculinity include physical strength and bravado, exclusive heterosexuality, stoicism, authority, and independence. This ideal is "embedded in religious doctrine and practice, mass media content, wage structures, the design of housing, welfare/taxation policies and so forth."[18] Connell emphasizes that hegemonic masculinity does not necessarily represent what "real" men are; in fact, movie stars are typically the only ones who fully embody the ideal:

> The public face of hegemonic masculinity is not necessarily what powerful men are, but what sustains their power and what large numbers of men are motivated to support. The notion of "hegemony" generally implies a large measure of consent. Few men are Bogarts or Stallones, many collaborate in sustaining those images.[19]

The most powerful groups in society control cultural production so that the most visible and pervasive forms and images of masculinity reaffirm their privilege. For the most part, these groups consist of wealthy white men, but to be successful, the forms they endorse must appeal to a wide range of men, including those who lack institutional power. As Susan Bordo points out, many men who are denied access to power (due to race, class, sexual orientation, or some other social reason), often accept and identify with the position and privileges associated with being male in a patriarchal culture.[20] Masculinity, then, is a cultural ideal that many men support, but do not necessarily embody.

According to Connell, the forms of masculinity change historically, depending on the dominant group's perception of their current material and emotional interests. In eighteenth century colonial America, for example, hegemonic masculinity stressed social usefulness, piety, and religious submission, in stark contrast to the current formulation of what it means to "be a man."[21] Thus, to paraphrase Marx, the dominant ideas about gender in any historical period are the ideas of the dominant gender—or at least those of the most powerful members of the dominant gender.

The concept of hegemonic masculinity acknowledges that there are competing definitions of masculinity. Indeed, the notion of hegemony always implies resistance. Connell argues that "alternative masculinities" coexist and directly compete with the dominant hegemonic forms. For example, during the 1960s, the dominant form of masculinity, represented by the "mature" male breadwinner with a steady job and a house in the suburbs, was challenged by "alternative" forms endorsed by the Beat subculture and later the hippie movement.[22] Currently, the ideal is contested by some groups of African-American men and gay men, who (for different reasons) do not conform to the breadwinner image still at the heart of hegemonic masculinity.[23] While individual men in these groups define themselves as "masculine," they may associate widely different qualities with this term. In fact, various meanings of masculinity always compete for preeminence. The version that ultimately achieves hegemonic status represents the interests of the most powerful members of our society, but its preeminence is always contested.

Thus, masculinity is an ideal that varies historically and culturally as different groups struggle over its meaning. However, all forms of masculinity have one characteristic in common: the imperative of being different from and superior to femininity. In other words, masculinity is always defined in opposition to femininity, regardless of the particular forms it takes.

This feature of masculinity can be detected crossculturally in the division of labor by gender. Using the image of the double helix, Margaret Higonnet and Patrice

Higonnet describe a consistent pattern in men's and women's work roles:

> The female strand on the helix is opposed to the male strand, and position on the female strand is subordinate to position on the male strand. The image of the double helix allows us to see that, although the roles of men and women vary greatly from culture to culture, their relationship is in some sense constant. If men gather and women fish, gathering will be thought more important than fishing; in another society where men fish and women gather, fishing will be more prestigious. The actual nature of the social activity is not as critical as the cultural perception of its relative value in a gender-linked structure of subordination.[24]

Regardless of its content—which varies historically and culturally—men's work is generally considered more powerful and prestigious than women's work.

Men typically support the gendered division of labor because they derive economic and social status from it. Moreover, supporting this division may satisfy the need many men currently feel to differentiate from and subordinate women and thus resolve the psychological conflicts identified by psychoanalytic theory.

In my view, this psychoanalytic theory of gender identity, combined with attention to the social and political context of male power, offers the most complete and compelling definition of masculinity available. According to psychoanalytic theory, the process of gender identity formation creates in men the desire to differentiate from and define themselves as superior to women. However, the particular forms of this desire in any historical and cultural setting depends on the interests of the most powerful members of the society, whose values and beliefs are always contested by other groups. The meaning of masculinity is constantly changing as a result of those struggles for dominance. But a consistent feature of all hegemonic forms is that masculinity is always defined as *different from* and *better than* women and femininity. Many men (but certainly not all men) support these forms for economic, social, *and* psychological reasons.

Feminist psychoanalytic theory, informed by Connell's concept of hegemonic masculinity, is a very useful tool for analyzing men's experiences in female occupations. These men are perceived as a threat to male differentiation and dominance, because they seem to upset the gendered division of labor (a key component of men's institutionalized power in society). For that reason, they are often represented as "anomalies" in popular culture and are accused of being effeminate and homosexual. Some of the men who work in these occupations may actually see themselves this way: They willingly embrace what Connell has called "alternative masculinities" that threaten the hegemonic form of masculinity.

But for many others, this accusation that they are not masculine makes no sense. They support and identify with hegemonic masculinity. But because their masculinity is not automatically vindicated through their jobs (as it may be for men who work in more traditional lines of work), they engage in various strategies to demarcate and distinguish themselves from their female colleagues. Their interests in doing so are in part economic and social—men are rewarded by the "glass escalator" for proving themselves masculine. But there is an irrational element to men's struggle to assert their difference and superiority, which may stem from the unconscious processes described by psychoanalytic theorists. At any rate, their efforts at "doing gender" often serve to reproduce the dominant social forms of masculinity, thereby sustaining men's gender privileges within these occupations.

Hegemonic Masculinity in Female Occupations

Waiting for a scheduled interview with a librarian, I had _____ the various clippings and announce-_____ door. In the center was a car-_____us, brutish, muscular man la-_____" (a takeoff on "Conan the _____ little doubt that the man _____e.

_____ategies to "maintain" heg-_____ occupations. Men dis-_____en in the workplace by _____tain male-identified spe-_____line elements of the job, _____positions, and disassoci-_____ Each of these strategies _____ of themselves as differ-_____—thus contributing to _____n from women in a way

_____al segregation of men _____fessions. Certain spe-_____s of men than others. _____o find male nurses in _____ychiatric wards than in obstetrical wards. Men are more likely to teach in the higher grades in elementary schools, whereas 98 percent of kindergarten teachers are women. School librarianship is also an overwhelmingly female specialty (over 95 percent female), but men make up over a third of all academic librarians. And caseworkers in social-work agencies are mostly women, while administrators and managers in those agencies are mostly men.[25]

Several of the men I interviewed claimed that they entered their particular specialties precisely because they contained more men. For example, one man left his job as a school social worker to work in a methadone drug treatment program because "I think there was some macho shit there [in myself], to tell you the truth, because I remember feeling a little uncomfortable there . . . ; it didn't feel right to me." Another social worker told me, "I think one of the reasons personally for me that I moved to corrections—and I think it was real unconscious—was the conflict [over masculinity]. I think corrections . . . is a little more macho than like if I worked in a child guidance clinic like I used to." For both of these men, specializing in "male-identified" areas helped them resolve inner conflicts about masculinity caused by being male in a predominantly female occupation.

The social workers I interviewed seemed much more self-consciously aware of specialization as a strategy for maintaining masculinity than members of the other professional groups (probably as a result of their professional training). Other men in the study were not quite so articulate in describing their psychological needs to differentiate from women, but they often made it clear during the course of the interviews that their specialties were chosen in part because they felt they were more appropriate for men. For instance, a psychiatric nurse chose his specialty "because psych is pretty easy for me. That's what I scored the highest in on the boards. And there's a lot more males, I think, in psych than on the floors. . . ."

And this sixth grade teacher explained his preference for teaching the upper grades:

> I felt I had a little more of an affinity for that age level. I could go down to fifth, but below fifth, they're just a little too cutesy, a little too young, and I get a little tired of explaining things seven or eight times. . . . I did [substitute teaching in] second grade three different times, and after that I said, "No more primaries." I think it was like that movie with Arnold Schwarzenegger, *Kindergarten Cop:* You think you have everything under control and things just fall apart. . . . I think at that age, the kids relate more effectively to a woman, you know, the mother figure. Cause that's more of a significant person in their lives at that age. That's the way I see it. And I think, I assume that that's why you don't see so many men teaching those grades.

It is significant that this teacher identifies with Arnold Schwarzenegger, an emblem of masculinity in our culture. This is how hegemonic masculinity works: It is not necessarily what men are, but a symbolic form that men are motivated to support. Arnold Schwarzenegger is a physically strong, stoic, and unambiguously heterosexual movie star. By identifying with him and his inability to control a kindergarten class, this teacher establishes a sense of himself as powerful and in control since he teaches the *sixth* grade—even though this is also a traditionally female occupation.

As argued in chapter 5, stratification within these professions is due in part to the "glass escalator": Men are channeled into specialties considered more legitimate for men, and many of them are complicit with this process. Internal stratification is due to a combination of organizational pressures and individual motives. This point was nicely summarized in an interview with a female social worker. When asked if her agency assigned men and women to different jobs, she quipped, "I heard never give some big buck a juvenile job unless he wants it. And if he wants it, he wouldn't say it anyways."

Emphasizing the Masculine

Specializing in male-identified areas is perhaps the most obvious way that men can differentiate themselves from women. However, even those who work in the more "traditional" female specialties can distinguish the work they do from "women's work" by highlighting the masculine aspects of their specialties.[20] School and public librarians, for example, can identify with automating the library catalogue and other computer work that they do. One public librarian specializing in cataloging believes that advanced technology was the key to attracting him as well as other men to the profession:

> After automation became part of the profession, more and more men are coming. I think that men are looking more for prestigious careers, and automation has given that to the profession. Not just organizing books, but applying technology in the process.

Another approach to emphasizing the masculine is to focus on the prestige of one's workplace. A California teacher who described his institution as "the top flight elementary school in the country" said,

> It makes you feel good about your job. It makes you, as a male, feel like it's okay to be a teacher, because this is a highly prestigious institution in the world of private schools.

Other men focused on the power and authority of their particular job specialties. Describing a previous job in Children's Protective Services (a heavily female specialty), this Arizona social worker said,

> Child welfare is an area in social work where you balance a helping role with a social control role. Going out to people's homes, I almost wore two hats: a social worker and an authority figure, someone with some enforcement power. . . . I carried a certain amount of professional and legal authority with me. . . . I literally had the authority to take people's kids out of their homes.

In addition, a few men emphasized the physical aspects of their work. A former teacher at a school for autistic children explained that men were needed for "restraining" the children, some of whom were "very, very violent." And a public librarian specializing in children's collections described a distinctive reading style he observed among the few male storytellers in town:

> I guess you could say, maybe in some sense, we're real physical in our storytimes, you know, the way we interact with the kids. I don't mean . . . I mean, these days, you have to be very careful touching children, of course. . . . I don't mean real touchy-feely, but I mean . . . you just get a real physical sense of the story.

Thus, men can identify with the technical or physical aspects of their jobs, or emphasize the special prestige or power that accrue to them because of their specific institutions. In all of these ways, men can highlight the components of their jobs that are consistent with hegemonic masculinity, thus maintaining a sense of themselves as "masculine" even though they work in nontraditional occupations.

This particular strategy of "emphasizing the masculine" is used when dealing with individuals outside the workplace. Some men told me that in certain contexts they rename their work to give it a more masculine, and hence more legitimate, connotation. For example, one social worker in private practice calls himself a "psychotherapist." A teacher tells those he meets at parties that he is "in education." A nurse introduces himself to new patients as "a former Vietnam combat nurse."[27] And a librarian told me that he is always selective about the contexts in which he reveals his occupation:

> At a "redneck" bar, I wouldn't sit down and drink a couple of beers and announce to the guy next to me with his gimme cap, "Hello, I'm a school librarian." He wouldn't care and he wouldn't be able to even think about a job like that. So it really depends on the audience. But the people I socialize with are people who are extremely understanding.

For these men, "naming" the occupation to the "wrong" audience could be threatening, so they rename their work, or describe it to "outsiders" in more masculine, and hence, more acceptable language.

The renaming of work is a common strategy in the labor force. In Rosemary Pringle's study of secretaries, she found that when men were employed to do this sort of work, they were usually called by some other name, such as "administrative assistant," "information officer," or "computer operator."[28] Both the bosses and the male workers colluded in this renaming, obscuring the actual similarity in men's and women's work. This practice of renaming no doubt exaggerates the degree of segregation in certain occupations, but it effectively maintains the perception that men and women have totally different workplace functions and abilities.[29]

This strategy of "emphasizing the masculine" also is employed by some men in their dealings with their female colleagues at work. Some men occasionally set themselves apart from women by refusing to participate in certain "feminine" activities. One teacher, for example, described how the only male teacher she worked with was very selective about his participation in school functions:

> Roland does fix all the projectors and he runs around ... and sets up science kits and stuff, but he's volunteered for that. There are other things that he claims he can't do as well. ... He never wants to be on a social committee, for example, or get plants when someone's ill, or collect for cards, for whatever reasons. Even picking up the staff room—he jokes that he has to have a cleaning lady at his house so he certainly doesn't want to be on the cleanup detail at school. So there are things that he doesn't do. But he makes up in other ways, because that's what he's gifted in and good at.
>
> [CW: And the teachers feel fine about that?]
>
> Oh, yeah.

In another example, a social worker who enjoyed socializing with his female colleagues (they even threw him a wedding shower) drew the line at bringing a covered dish to the office "pot luck" parties:

> I told them I wasn't making any. We have pot lucks for our Christmas party, and picnics for the [foster] children. But I informed them that now that I'm married, I had no intention of changing that either.

I bring potato chips or Kool-Aid, something that's very easy and takes no work. The rest of the women make something.

These are subtle ways that men can informally set themselves apart from their female colleagues. By picking and choosing among various informal activities in the workplace, men can carve a "masculine" niche for themselves among their female peers.

A more extreme type of this differentiation is the formation of groups that exclude women. Sometimes this segregation is informal, and conducted in a spirit of joking and camaraderie, as in the case of this public library:

[CW: How would you describe relations between the male and female staff in your department?]

Well, it's hard to say. I don't think it really comes up as a male-female thing. There's a gang of people, and you're one of the gang. We joke once in a while when the situation [arises] when all four of us on the [reference] desk are all male or female. We say, "Well, the macho crew is on tonight. You know, we're going to sit out there in our t-shirts and spit on the floor." It's just in joking. . . .

[CW: So there's not a sense of "we versus they"?]

No. It may break down that way, I guess, when we come up here [to the staff lounge] and eat dinner. You might find females congregate on one table, and talk about things they'll typically talk about, and males may do the same thing. But I think when we're in our back workroom, we talk about whatever library issues, or personal things. . . . I don't see it as segregation.

But there were a few instances of men segregating themselves in a more formal and intentional manner. This teacher described the formation of a "men's club" at his school:

> There are some men teachers who I feel are very insecure. One time a teacher formed a "men's club," a male teacher. It was to do "manly" kinds of things. [laughs]
>
> [CW: Like to change tires or something? (laughs)]
>
> No, it was to get together and preserve the idea that we are men in this profession and there are a lot of women here, and let's just get together and have a drink, or have breakfast. It was sort of tongue-in-cheek in a lot of ways. But sometimes it wasn't. And I would not be a member of the club. I refused to be a member of the club, for that reason, that weirdness. It's hard to articulate it. . . . Some of the things I could joke and go along with, but other things I could not. . . .

This kindergarten teacher felt ambivalent about the "men's club": On the one hand, he felt it important to recognize that men are a numerical minority within the teaching profession, and that they have special interests and concerns as men (such as dealing with the suspicion that they are pedophiles). But he was uncomfortable with the "weirdness" in this club, which he linked to the organizer's insecurity about his masculinity. Those who have studied all-male organizations have also identified a fundamental insecurity about masculinity as their basis.[30] The exclusion of women from "clubs" is usually an attempt to distinguish men from women and establish men's dominance over women. Anthropologist Peggy Reeves Sanday, who has studied all-male groups in several societies, writes,

> Cross-cultural research demonstrates that whenever men build and give allegiance to a mystical, enduring, all-male social group, the disparagement of women is, invariably, an important ingredient of the mystical bond, and sexual aggression the means by which the bond is renewed.[31]

Sanday argues that because we live in a sexist society, all-male groups inevitably perpetuate male differentiation and domination over women—the probable source of the "weirdness" identified by this teacher.

The "men's club" is perhaps an extreme example of men's attempts to differentiate from women. But it is an example of a common strategy to "emphasize the masculine" employed by men in the "women's professions." This general strategy also includes men focusing on certain technical or prestigious elements of their jobs, renaming their work to outsiders, and segregating themselves from their female colleagues. Each of these activities undermines any challenge to hegemonic masculinity represented by men who work in predominantly female jobs.

Administration and Higher Educational Credentials

A third distancing strategy is to define the present occupation as a way station for future jobs that are more lucrative, prestigious, or challenging (and thus more legitimate for men). Men who use this strategy do not identify with their current jobs, but see them as laying the groundwork for future jobs. For instance, a teacher told me that he chose to start his career in elementary school to "learn the basics of human nature," and then move up to junior high, and ultimately high school (where there is a much larger proportion of men). Others saw their professions as "springboards" to other careers. An Arizona nurse, for example, who saw "nursing as a backup," hoped in the future to work in the biomedical engineering profession.

Aspiring to the top rungs of the profession was an especially common distancing strategy. Men described future plans to become "director of a branch library" (children's librarian), "director of a home for the aged" (floor nurse), or a "principal of a school" (fourth grade teacher). These areas were all explicitly defined as more appropriate for men, and they are also viewed as more prestigious and powerful than rank-and-file jobs.

As is the case in most professions, advancement to these top positions often requires higher educational preparation beyond the entry-level credential. Men are more likely than women to seek postgraduate degrees in these occupations. As table 5 indicates, the higher the educational credential, the higher the proportion of men earning the degree. Indeed, men received nearly half of the doctorates awarded in education and library science in 1988.

This discrepancy in the representation of men and women in postcredential degree programs is due to a number of factors. First, men are often encouraged to "aim high" by mentors simply because they are men (see chapter 5). A Massachusetts nurse was told by his first clinical instructor in his associate degree (ADN) program,

> "You've got to go on. You *have* to go on . . . past the ADN," she said. "You have to; you are a man." She said, "You have to get more men into the profession; we need men."

Thus, men may receive more encouragement than women to reach the top of their professions.

A second reason for men's overrepresentation among

Table 5
*Number of Bachelor's, Master's, and Doctoral
Degrees Conferred, and Percentage Received by Men,
by Field of Study, 1987–1988*

Field of Study	Bachelor's		Master's		Doctoral	
	Total	% Men	Total	% Men	Total	% Men
Nursing	31,567	5.1	6,400	7.4	283	9.5
Education	91,013	23.1	77,704	24.9	6,544	45.0
Library Science	123	13.8	3,713	21.3	46	47.8
Social Work	8,471	13.8	9,344	18.6	226	39.4

SOURCE: National Center for Education Statistics, *Digest of Education Statistics, 1990* (Washington, D.C.: Government Printing Office, 1991), table 224, pp. 236–43.

higher degree recipients and administrative officeholders involves men's and women's different family obligations. Women often shoulder the primary responsibility for household care, even when they are employed full-time. This frees up married men to dedicate themselves more exclusively to pursuing higher educational credentials and higher administrative positions.[32] I interviewed three men whose spouses were in the same profession as they, and each had a higher degree than his wife. A doctoral student in library science, who met his wife in the master's degree program, explained why he pursued an advanced degree and she did not:

> I realized that I have the responsibility to become the provider at home. . . . She thought that if she were comfortable, if she found a nice [work] environment, she didn't need to go further [with her education]. She didn't have to push harder. . . . And during the time we were in college, the family was

growing. So the demand for her to stay at home and care for the kids was growing, too.

Overall, women are far more likely than men to drop out of the labor force. Nearly half of all women in the work force drop out for at least one six-month period, compared to 13 percent of all men.[33] And when women do drop out, it is usually for family reasons: In 1990, 62 percent of the women who had left the labor force for an extended period claimed that they were "keeping house"; only 3 percent of the men who dropped out gave the same reason.[34]

The fact that women drop out of the labor force to care for their children is frequently cited as the main reason why men predominate in the upper echelons of these professions. For instance, the nursing director of a hospital emergency room (ER) explained why men are overrepresented in the top positions:

> The men sometimes tend to be a little more stable than the women. A lot of the men who work in the ER have really been here for quite a while. They're married. Most have kids. But when it's time to have a baby, they're not the ones who take off. It's the same problem, it's not a lot different than a lot of other professions. . . . All the men [nurses] we've got here who are married to nurses and have children, without exception, it's been their wives that have taken the flex options and the men have stayed working forty hours.

Professions tend to reward those who follow a specific pattern of career development: early training, continuous employment, technical as opposed to interpersonal skill acquisition, few competing family responsibilities. Men conform more easily to this pattern in part because of the

widespread cultural expectation that men should priori-
tize their career interests over their family roles. As Catharine MacKinnon has argued, professional standards are
not "gender neutral," but rather, "[men's] socially designed biographies define workplace expectations and
successful career patterns."[35] Of course, this doesn't mean
that women are incapable of following this "male" career
pattern by, for example, forgoing marriage and family to
escape competing obligations. But women are disadvan-
taged as a group because the criteria for success and promotion even in these predominantly female occupations
favor the male model of labor force participation.

Thus, men have more opportunities and receive more
encouragement than women to seek the top positions in
these occupations. But aside from these two structural
reasons, men often have personal motives, linked to their
desire to be masculine, to strive for the top. Achieving
success is a way they can maintain their masculinity in a
female occupation. For example, a social worker employed in the mental health services department of a large
urban area, reflected on his move into administration:

> The more I think about it, through our discussion,
> I'm sure that's a large part of why I wound up in
> administration. It's okay for a man to do the admin-
> istration. In fact, I don't know if I fully answered a
> question that you asked a little while ago about how
> did being male contribute to my advancing in the
> field. I was saying it wasn't because I got any special
> favoritism as a man, but . . . I think . . . because I'm
> a man, I felt a need to get into this kind of position.
> I may have worked harder toward it, may have com-
> peted harder for it, than most women would do, even
> women who think about doing administrative work.

For many men, pursuing administrative positions is a
way of "distancing" themselves from women, carving a

masculine niche for themselves, and thus establishing more legitimacy for their presence in these female occupations.

Part of what motivates this particular strategy for maintaining masculinity is competition with other men. A clinical social worker at a university hospital described why he decided to pursue a doctorate:

> First of all, even though most of the social workers there were women, most of the people [at the hospital where he worked] were men, especially the psychiatrists and psychologists. . . . Most of my friends were . . . male . . . who were psychology or psychiatry interns or residents. . . . And I think it just got to me, or motivated me, or a sense of competition, or something, but seeing each new cohort move on to getting their degree and moving on to something bigger and better, I just felt that I ought to do the same. . . . I decided to apply either to law school or for a doctorate in social work or psychology.

Those men I interviewed who worked alongside other professional men with better paid and more prestigious credentials felt an enormous amount of pressure to advance their own education. A former LVN who was taken under the wing of a prominent research physician explained why he was motivated to eventually pursue a master's degree in nursing:

> Because I was always working with people with Ph.D.'s, with M.D.'s, or with RN behind their name— BSN, MSN [Bachelor's and Master's of Science in Nursing]—it really served as a catalyst. That was it, I had to get back to school.

This nurse's experience illustrates the combination of organizational pressures and individual desires motivating many men in these professions. His pursuit of higher degrees was motivated in part by the unusual opportunity he was given to publish and do research as an LVN, and in part by his personal desire to make himself an equal to the other men at work. Greater opportunities for men, combined with their psychological desire to identify with the higher-status males (and disassociate from women) encourage them to strive for advancement instead of remaining, as another director of social work services put it, "just a social worker."

Of course, women also pursue advanced degrees and careers in administration. But the women I interviewed did not pursue advanced degrees as a distancing strategy. This emphasis on competing for prestige was missing from their accounts of their motivations. Indeed, in one case, a respondent entered a doctoral program because she thought that college teaching would be more accommodating to her family obligations:

> If I look back, I think that really the most satisfying times in my career was when I had my master's degree and I supervised in child welfare. . . . I think I saw coming back to get my Ph.D. as a way to teach at the university level and have a different, more flexible schedule when I was raising my child. I really kind of looked at it as the means to have a certain kind of lifestyle.

It is not the case that women in these professions lack ambition, or that they "fear success."[36] Rather, my interviews suggest that many men in these professions are "hyperambitious" in part because of their psychological need to distance themselves from the work of women. Pursuing higher degrees and administrative positions are strategies they use to reproduce masculinity in female occupations.

Disassociation

The final distancing strategy used by the men in this study was disassociation from their work. Some men feel little or no connection to their jobs: They either fell into their professions with little forethought or planning, or they became gravely disaffected by their work once they began their careers.[37] For example, a public librarian explained why he chose his profession:

> I sort of thought that it wouldn't be too stressful, it wouldn't be too hard. You could go anywhere in the country you wanted to and get a job. To a small town or something, which certainly has an appeal. Since there's a lot of women, you could do things like take a year off and come back, and people wouldn't look at your résumé and say, "What is that? What is this year off?" And you wouldn't be required to climb a career ladder.

This man described himself as entirely lacking in ambition and enthusiasm for the librarianship profession, and mocked others who took their jobs more seriously.

Similarly, a teacher told me that he got his teaching certificate in college because "it was always something I figured I could fall back on. Or if I moved, I could always get a teaching position if something else didn't work out." Currently he is working on a second degree to become an exercise physiologist, and he plans to continue teaching "only as long as it takes me to get out of there."

Part of this disassociation strategy is to condemn or deride others who are in the profession—particularly other men. A public librarian described his male co-workers as "a bit old ladyish because they've worked in reference a long time. I don't know if that's because of their personality or working in a job so many years. Just being sort of nervous." He explained that he has remained in the same position for nineteen years only because he loves living in Cambridge—not because of his job. And a social worker who periodically leaves his profession to pursue other interests (including a yearlong stint as a card dealer in Atlantic City), described his male colleagues in less-than-glowing terms:

> I grew up in the world of work, business, the bottom line. There is not that kind of accountability in social work. My stereotype of men coming into social work is maybe this is easier, they don't want to face the real world where you're going to be held accountable.

By condemning the profession—and the other men in it— men can distance themselves from their work, and preserve a sense of themselves as different and better than those employed in these professions.

Sometimes this disassociation strategy is directed toward gay men in these professions. Some straight men deride their gay colleagues, blaming them for the poor status of their work. In an interview study of male nurses by Joel Heikes, several men expressed extremely homophobic attitudes.[38] I did not find ample evidence of homophobia in my interviews, perhaps because men are less comfortable expressing anti-gay sentiments to a woman interviewer. However, several of the men I interviewed did make it perfectly clear that they were straight, apparently to distinguish themselves from their gay colleagues (and the gay stereotype about men who work in these professions). Since heterosexuality is a key component of hegemonic masculinity, this disassociation strategy allows men to maintain a sense of themselves as appropriately masculine even though they work in predominantly female jobs.

Thus, men can use several strategies to maintain their masculinity in these female occupations: They can differentiate themselves from women by specializing in certain male-identified areas, by emphasizing masculine components of their jobs, by aspiring to higher administrative positions, and by disassociating from their professions altogether. Each of these strategies entails establishing difference from and superiority over women. Thus, paradoxically, men in nontraditional occupations can and do actually support hegemonic masculinity, and end up posing little threat to the social organization of gender.

Alternative Masculinities

A few of the men in this study do not support hegemonic masculinity. These men reject the dominant society's expectations of what men should be, and they view their careers in nontraditional professions as a manifestation of their "alternative" perspectives. They articulate what Connell calls "alternative masculinities"; that is, their ideas about manhood conflict with the hegemonic ideas that men should be powerful, stoic, economically successful, and heterosexual.

Some of the gay men I interviewed were among those rejecting hegemonic masculinity.[39] For example, a California social worker told me that, as a gay man, his "masculinity and identity are in no way tied in with my having to be in a male-oriented job." In fact, he believed that the social work profession attracted him in part because it could accommodate the perspectives of marginal individuals who were "outsiders" to the dominant society's norms and values. He said,

> I spent my whole life working on understanding dif-
> ferences because of my own. And therefore I think I
> have both been gravitated toward [social work] and
> have perhaps a capacity to deal with that. . . . I think
> the people who don't have to deal with differences,
> whatever that is, end up being perhaps in more ster-
> eotypical kinds of roles, be it in a marriage or be it
> a profession.

Although this respondent did identify certain stereotypically masculine traits within himself (such as competi-
tiveness), he viewed his career choice as a conscious—
and to some extent unconscious—rejection of socially
sanctioned masculinity.

A few of the heterosexual men I interviewed also considered their occupational choice a rejection of socially
prescribed masculinity. A California librarian who described himself as "a hippie artist in San Francisco" before entering the profession, rejected the stereotypical
roles of men and women:

> I knew the pay [in librarianship] was low. And I
> didn't give a damn about stuff like that. That's the
> legacy of the sixties, not a legacy of me being a man
> or a woman, or anything else. People of my partic-
> ular generation and outlook were led to believe that
> satisfying work was what counted. If you were true
> to yourself, and found satisfying work, all the other
> things would follow along.

In his case, he does not think of himself as a librarian to
this day. In his mind, "I was an artist first. I still am an
artist first." Librarianship pays his salary to support his
"true" vocation, which he identifies with the artist coun-
terculture, and the rejection of the traditional male
breadwinner role.

Very few men in my sample viewed themselves as "gender renegades," however, and those who did often expressed considerable ambivalence. For instance, one Massachusetts teacher claimed that entering elementary education inspired in him "a lot of feelings about being male in a nontraditional role that made me feel good about my job, made me feel that I was a bit of a rebel, that I was breaking the mold. . . . I just felt good about being different." Yet, since entering the profession, he has faced increasing pressure to enter administration, in part because of his own desire to live up to the male provider role in his family. Near the end of the interview he told me,

> The rebel side of me still wants to ignore all the rules about success. But, hey, it's hard. I've got a brother-in-law who's going to be earning a six-figure salary soon, and that's my wife's sister who's going to be living in the big, white home in the suburbs, vacationing all over the world. And we're going to be looking forward to our trip to the beach in August. That's hard. It's hard for me. It's not necessarily hard for my wife, but it's really hard for me. . . . When I compare myself to other men in my age cohort now, it's a pretty . . . devastating picture.

Indeed, many of the men in these "nontraditional" occupations described inexorable pressures to conform to hegemonic masculine norms. As I indicated in chapter 5, some of this pressure emanates from the structures of the occupations which encourage men to succeed despite their intentions. But men also experience internal psychological pressures to conform, which are at least as daunting as the "glass escalator."

Conclusion

Men working in traditionally female occupations symbolize a challenge to—if not an outright rejection of—masculinity. Picture a male nurse, librarian, elementary school teacher, or social worker. The image that comes to mind is probably not a hypermasculine Rambo-type of man, but a softer, more effeminate man.

Some of the men in these occupations do consider themselves "gender renegades" who reject society's proscriptions about how men ought to behave. But most of the men in this study work very hard to differentiate themselves from women and femininity. Even men who appear to be living embodiments of a gender revolution often insist that men and women are completely different. For instance, a nursing professor who told me his "nurturing and caring values were higher than most people's"—he devotes his summers to working as a regular floor nurse to hone his caring skills—nevertheless firmly believes that men are more rational than women, and men are more committed than women to career advancement. He said, "The sexes do think differently. There is a genetic component." The belief in dichotomous gender differences can survive occupational integration.

Men who work in nursing, teaching, librarianship, and social work have a lot at stake in maintaining their masculinity. The economic and status advantages men receive in these occupations may be contingent on successfully presenting an image of themselves as both different from and better than women. And for many men, establishing a subjective sense of their masculine identity requires that they distinguish themselves from women.

For the men in these occupations, convincing themselves and others that they are appropriately masculine is an uphill battle because of the stereotypes that surround men who do "women's work." Men in more traditional "male" occupations probably face a less formidable struggle to demonstrate that they are masculine. Occupational segregation historically has been a guaranteed means used by men to maintain their masculinity. This has been one of the reasons why men have been very reluctant to allow women into their occupations: The prospect of job integration threatens men because it challenges their automatic claims to privilege that they have been socialized to desire, and which many expect as their birthright. Indeed, some social commentators claim that there is a contemporary "crisis of masculinity" due to the large-scale entry of women into the labor force.[40] The enormous growth in popularity of the mythopoetic "men's movement" as spearheaded by Robert Bly attests to many men's desperate search for new ways to distinguish themselves from women. Their desire to "get in touch" with their masculinity probably stems from feeling increasingly undifferentiated from women. The mythopoetic "men's movement" reassures men (with readymade, male-only rituals) that they can still be "men" in this integrated (and, some fear, female-dominated) society.[41]

The men in these female occupations may be in the vanguard of looking for ways to be "men" in integrated workplaces. Their strategies for doing this vary, but each enables them to maintain an image of themselves as different from women and superior to them. Ironically, they support "hegemonic masculinity" in spite of their nontraditional roles.

7

Occupational Segregation and Gender Inequality

Occupational segregation by gender is a major social problem for working women. Full-time working women earn less than three-quarters of what full-time working men earn, and at least 40 percent of this wage gap is due to women's concentration in lesser-paying jobs.[1] Occupational segregation also perpetuates the limitations imposed by gender stereotypes. Women are typecast as caring and "expressive" personalities in part because of their service-oriented jobs, while men are believed to be more technically proficient and more competent decision-makers because of the kinds of jobs they hold.[2] If equal numbers of men and women were employed as mechanics, managers, and airplane pilots, as well as nurses, librarians, and secretaries, these stereotypes would be far more difficult to sustain. Occupational segregation also has negative personal costs, insofar as it impedes individuals' pursuit of satisfying and fulfilling work. For all of these reasons, occupational segregation ought to be eliminated: People should not be prevented from taking any job because of their gender.

However, even with a strong commitment to ending occupational segregation by gender, some feminists remain wary of men's entry into predominantly female occupations. For example, Linda Blum expresses trepidation about this prospect because she fears that men would take over the best jobs and displace women workers. She further claims that occupational segregation might even "protect" women workers during periods of economic decline. Because women workers are often the first fired when layoffs occur, it may be best, she writes, "to maintain an occupational arena where women do not compete directly with men."[3] As long as there is gender inequality and discrimination in the wider society, Blum cautions against endorsing whole-scale integration without considering its consequences for the *women* concentrated in predominantly female jobs.

Clearly, this study confirms that men's integration into women's jobs does not overtly challenge status hierarchies based on gender. We have seen that men tend to be concentrated in the more prestigious and better-paying job specialties. Part of this inequality is caused by what I call "the glass escalator"—the structural features of these professions that enhance men's careers independent of their ambition or desire. The gender inequality in these professions also stems from a psychological dynamic men bring with them into these jobs. Men have both psychological and material incentives to distinguish themselves from women, resulting in the reproduction of gender hierarchy within these occupations (see chapter 6).

Consequently, whether more men should be encouraged to seek employment in nursing, teaching, librarianship, and social work is an open question. In the grand scheme of things, this occupational integration is a noble and worthy goal. But in the present context of an unequal society that privileges men over women, we ought to abide Blum's caveats and carefully assess the consequences of integration for women and gender inequality.

This chapter explores the various meanings and consequences of job integration for those working in nursing, teaching, librarianship, and social work. In the first part of the chapter, I examine views about whether or not more men are needed in these professions. Respondents were divided on this question, and even those who endorsed the hiring of more men disagreed about the reasons for doing so. Some framed their responses in terms of the ultimate goal of gender equality, but others drew upon stereotypes of gender differences to justify the inclusion of more men. I argue that these beliefs about gender could further entrench inequality between men and women because gender differentiation tends to benefit men.

The second part of the chapter examines the different strategies proposed to encourage more men to enter these fields. Men and women gave two main reasons why men are so underrepresented in these professions: the feminine identification of the work, and the low pay of the work. Depending on which factor they emphasized, different policies were recommended to change the gender imbalance of their professions. I argue that many of the policies recommended to encourage men to enter predominantly female occupations could easily reproduce men's advantages. In particular, policies intended to help women enter and succeed in "male professions" could unintentionally preserve male privilege if applied to men in the "women's professions."

Ending segregation within the "women's professions" is not nearly as clear-cut an issue as ending segregation in the male professions. Getting women into "men's jobs" promises to enhance women's economic and social status, so most everyone committed to gender equity supports policies that will facilitate this transition. But increasing the number of men who do "women's work" is likely to reproduce gender hierarchy and male privilege unless a strategy that will not be oppressive to women can be identified.

Should There Be More Men?

My respondents were divided on the question of whether there should be more men employed in these professions. While some men joked that more men were not needed because they did not want the "competition," others believed the need for more men in these professions was so dire, that affirmative action hiring guidelines favoring men ought to be instituted.

Among those expressing little concern about hiring more men were people employed in male-dominated specialties who did not perceive any gender imbalance needing correction. Indeed, in one case, a director of nursing worried that too *many* men were being hired for the most interesting and challenging jobs:

> [CW: Do you make any special effort to make sure that men are represented among the nurses? Or is gender not an issue when it comes to hiring?]

> It's an issue in that sometimes we have too many men and not enough women. . . . In the flight nurse program, we only have one female flight nurse now. There's a male chief flight nurse, and among the four

staff flight nurses, three of them are male and one is a woman. And I'm a little uncomfortable with that.

[CW: How do you account for [the overrepresentation of males in that area]?]

Well, it's a competitive process. There's a lot of people that apply. . . . A lot of men are attracted to that. Given that role, there may be a tendency to hire men instead of women. So it's kind of interesting, in a female-dominated profession, making sure you don't get into some discrimination against females.

At the upper levels at least, few argued that efforts should be undertaken to recruit more men. Several expressed more concern about the underrepresentation of women in the higher positions than about the low overall proportions of men in these occupations.[4]

Others responded to the question of whether there should be more men by saying that gender should not matter at all. A Massachusetts librarian said, "I really don't care if there are more men or more women in the profession. I only care that there are people in the profession who love it and do it well." And a social worker in Arizona responded,

I would say no, not necessarily. If we're moving toward a society where gender really doesn't make that much of a difference, it really shouldn't make that much difference. I don't know what men would bring to social work that's not already there.

Some of those who argued that gender does not matter maintained that *race* matters more. According to the 1980 U.S. Census, black men and women constitute 7 percent of all nurses and librarians, 11 percent of all elementary school teachers, and 19 percent of all social workers.[5] In the past, African Americans were underrepresented in each of these professions because of the "professionalization" efforts undertaken at the turn of the century (see chapter 2). In the nineteenth century, people of color and of lesser means were barred from these jobs as part of the attempt to heighten the status and respectability of these occupations. Throughout the twentieth century, each of these professions has grappled with its legacy of racial/ethnic exclusion, and each has attempted (with varying degrees of commitment) to recruit more minority group members.[6] For many respondents, redressing the racial imbalance was a far more important priority than attracting more men into their professions.

On the other hand, several respondents did strongly endorse recruiting and hiring more men. People gave three sets of reasons for wanting more men: personal reasons relating to the enhancement of workplace culture, social reasons relating to the betterment of society, and professional reasons concerning pay and status issues.

First, many men thought that their workplaces would be more congenial and they would be less lonely if they had more male colleagues. For example, a social worker described his feelings of loneliness and isolation at work:

> I really do have the feeling of being by myself. Some of it is just fluff stuff. I mean, like, "I went to the ball game last night." My colleagues could care less. Now some women like baseball; I happen to work with three who don't. Or, "I went fishing on my vacation." I have three colleagues who don't fish.

It was not uncommon for the men in this study to lament the lack of sports or "sports talk" at work. A school librarian explained why he preferred working in more integrated environments:

> I do enjoy the company of males as well as females, but it's fun to go in and do male things. Let's face it, I enjoy football results. I enjoy playing ball with one of my buddies. I enjoy shooting a basketball after school with two or three of the men (although the female P.E. teacher can play with us—she's great).

And a teacher admitted he would like his school to hire more men because then "we would have a better volleyball team."

Sports may seem like a trivial issue, but in these examples sports symbolize a kind of intimacy between men. Scott Swain has argued that sports are a major arena used by men to express their feelings and connections with other men. By participating in or talking about sports, Swain claims that "men can implicitly demonstrate closeness without directly verbalizing the relationship."[7] He argues that verbal intimacy, which is common between female friends, is far more threatening to men in their friendships with other men, so many use sports as a vehicle for expressing their feelings to each other. Thus, in the above cases, the desire for sports talk at work may symbolize a desire for intimacy with other men.

On the other hand, we have seen that the desire for more intimate contact with male colleagues may also be linked to the need to differentiate from women and establish superiority over them. Clearly this was the case for those who started the "men's club" (see chapter 6). A Texas teacher who wanted "three men in every elementary school," explained his preference for working with men in these terms:

> Men are kind of gregarious; there's a herd instinct or something. They like to be where other men are. They feel real uncomfortable when there's not other men around.

Thus, the desire for more male colleagues may also reflect a personal need to express one's solidarity with other men in opposition to women.[8]

In addition to these personal reasons for wanting more male colleagues, respondents cited various social reasons why more men should be recruited into their professions. A few believed that having more men in these fields would contribute to the breakdown of destructive gender stereotypes. For instance, a school librarian said that more men were "definitely" needed "to show children that the world is made up of people, human beings, and whether they're male or female doesn't make a whole lot of difference." And when asked why he thought there should be more men in teaching, a teacher told me,

> First, I think it's good because I don't think that any kind of a position should have traditional sex roles attached to it. I think that's real damaging, in any position, no matter what it is. . . . Secondly, I think it's real important for boys to see that men can perform jobs where a great deal of sensitivity and caring are involved and can still be the other side of that, you know, male.

However, not everyone advocated the entry of more men into these professions in order to transform gender roles. In fact, several said that more men were needed because of the special qualities they would bring *as men* to professional practice. For instance, a few said that men were better equipped than women to handle violent or dangerous situations at work. An Arizona social worker told me:

> Working with young males, and males in general, I think a man is very effective. And also dealing with dysfunctional families that have a male in it. Be-

cause, for one thing, if the father is alcoholic or abusive, they feel they can intimidate the female social worker. She has some barriers to cross before she can become effective. Whereas a man will react differently to men. Maybe he [a male social worker] doesn't have to overcome the testing that a female social worker has to go through.

Others maintained that more men were needed in social work because women social workers were reluctant to work with potentially violent populations, such as sex offenders and homeless drug addicts.

In addition to their special aptitudes, some argued that men contribute technical skills to their professional practice. According to a kindergarten teacher:

I think males bring in different interests in the classroom. Usually there's more of an interest in science and math in a man's classroom. . . . The few men that are in kindergarten always seem to be more "hands-on" science oriented although there are female teachers that do that too. But I think male teachers in younger grades tend to do more of that.

And discussing his function as a role model for young men, a public librarian who formerly worked in the "young adults" section of the library, said,

I helped people with their car problems. . . . We used to have young kids come into the library just to get the specifications for an automobile. The south branch library is located in a kind of working-class neighborhood, so kids, teenagers would come to the library just for an auto-repair manual. . . . I was able to give them lots of information.

According to this man, the growth of single-parent families has forced many boys to turn to outsiders for basic instruction in car and home repair that they otherwise would have received from their fathers. In his mind, male librarians are able to fulfill this "father" function, and more are needed to contribute such essential service to the community.

The need for men to serve as "role models" for male children was a recurring theme in the interviews. Teachers and social workers were particularly adamant about the need for men to work with children, especially those from single-parent homes or violent homes. Men in these professions could act as "surrogate fathers," providing young males with positive images of adult manhood to counteract their troubled family lives. A female teacher in California stated this point directly:

> I do think there are numerous rambunctious boys who don't have male models that need to have male teachers. We need more of them. We don't have enough of them. If your study is dealing with why don't men go into this profession, and how could they help [encourage more men], yes, it's right on target. We need many more.

Clearly, then, not everyone advocating the entry of more men into these professions felt that doing so posed a challenge to traditional gender distinctions. Many thought men would bring their special skills and orientations as men to their practice. Indeed, those who wanted more men in their professions often articulated a kind of "multi-culturalism" perspective, summarized by a public librarian in Arizona:

> It's good to have a range of public servants in any institution, any public service institution that represents the public. You get all sides. The same reason it's important to have a mixture of races and ages,

too. It just works better, I think. I wish there were more [men]. I think it would be good.

His argument was that men and women have different perspectives and abilities, and both should be duly and amply represented in these professions.

Thus, many respondents advocated more men entering their professions because of the positive social consequences they perceived would result from this integration. Although some thought that increasing integration of these professions would result in the diminishment of gender stereotypes, others drew upon those stereotypes to justify the recruitment of more men. In the latter case, gender difference provided the rationale for workplace integration.

Ironically, instead of challenging gender inequality, integration on these terms may actually perpetuate it. Each of these "masculine" qualities is amply rewarded by these professions, contributing to the "glass escalator effect" that enhances men's careers. Furthermore, these stereotypes disadvantage those who reject hegemonic masculine norms: If only those who possess these masculine qualities are recruited and rewarded, those who fail to (or refuse to) live up to these expectations will continue to encounter suspicion and possible exclusion.

A third set of reasons given for recruiting more men involves issues concerning professionalization. Recalling the arguments made by professional associations in the 1960s, several respondents argued that the status and pay of these fields would increase with the recruitment of more men. For instance, a nurse described the positive consequences of integration for nurse-physician relationships:

I think some physicians tend to treat the men [nurses] a little bit more as equal partners. . . .

There's both a positive and a negative side to that in that it sometimes offends the female nurses that that happens. And I understand that. On the other hand, I wonder if that's not maybe a little bit good for nursing. I generally feel like [male- or female-dominated] jobs are not a good idea. I feel that the more women we have in medicine, and more men we have in nursing, the issues will become more medical issues and nursing issues, and less male and female. And I can't see any downside to that. And I think the end result will be good for nursing.

Some men attributed the welcome they received in these predominantly female occupations to the general interest in increasing professional prestige. A librarian who noted that "librarians in general seem to have this prestige fixation that they're worried about," gave this reason for his positive reception in graduate school:

I think that it was viewed as perhaps being a good thing that men were becoming involved in the profession, that this might be a way to increase the prestige and/or level of remuneration. It would bring up the pay scale and would open doors and create opportunities.

It is true that salaries are positively correlated with the proportion of men in an occupation: In general, the more men in an occupation, the higher the salary. But the reasons for this phenomenon are fairly complex. Barbara Reskin and Patricia Roos have studied formerly "male" occupations that now include substantial proportions of women (including pharmacy, banking, and bartending).[9] They found that "feminizing" occupations such as these are characterized by declining value and rewards relative to other occupations that demand comparable training and effort. In other words, the proportion of women increases in an occupation only when that occupation is in decline. When occupations change for the worse, men simply leave them and go on to greener pastures, and women move in to fill the vacated positions.

Reskin and Roos use a theory of "queuing" to explain this historical pattern in occupational sex segregation. They suggest that workers are lined up in an imaginary "queue" organized by gender and race. Employers (who are mostly white men) prefer to hire white men. But when their jobs do not successfully attract ample numbers of white male applicants (due to competition from other employers), they move down the queue, selecting white women and racial/ethnic minority men and women who usually accept these jobs because their employment options are far more limited.

This theory can help explain why occupations with higher proportions of men tend to have higher salaries. Because white men are the preferred workers, they have their pick of the best jobs. According to Reskin and Roos, white male workers have the unique advantage of being able to "vote their preferences with their feet, relocating to new occupations that offer better prospects."[10]

Several of those who advocated hiring more men to increase the salaries of their professions sensed that men can command higher salaries and better treatment than women for precisely this reason. For example, an Arizona nurse argued:

> A lot of nurses will put up with situations that aren't workable. And I think men are a little more verbose and say, "No, I'm not dealing with that situation. And I'm going to go here [leave this job] if you don't provide this." And I don't know if we're directly responsible for wages increasing, but I think it has some-

thing to do with it. Same with the profession changing, becoming more flexible. . . . The people in power, whoever they may be, go "Oh, yeah. Gee, twenty patients—that is kind of hard. No lunch? No breaks? Huh, that is kind of unrealistic." And they'll go, "Okay, you can have a break." I think men will demand more.

Based on his experience, male nurses are more demanding than female nurses, and employers are more likely to heed their demands. If they did not, then men would simply "vote with their feet" and leave for more lucrative and rewarding positions elsewhere.

But why are employers willing to pay more money to hire and retain white men? Reskin and Roos argue that this is because most employers are themselves white men, and their economic decisions are made with an eye to preserving their race and gender privilege. They write that "employers tend to place greater weight on custom, stereotypes about sex differences in productivity, and anti-female or pro-male biases than they place on minimizing wages."[11]

Paying higher wages for white men is also consistent with a longstanding cultural tradition in this country. Alice Kessler-Harris has traced the history of pay inequality in the United States in a book of essays entitled *A Woman's Wage*.[12] She demonstrates that the different wages paid to male and female workers reflect a dominant belief among employers that men need more money than women do because they support families on their incomes. A "woman's wage" is less than a man's because employers presume that women are supported in part by their families. Recall that this was one of the reasons women were originally recruited for these jobs in the nineteenth century: Civic leaders believed that women would cost less to employ because they did not "need" the money. This same belief is still held by many people today. Although most women now (as then) need their incomes to support themselves and their families, this ideology is used to justify employers' discriminatory hiring and pay practices, and it contributes to the wage gap that disadvantages women in *every* occupation.

A few administrators interviewed for this study provided examples of what employers sometimes do to attract and retain men. An assistant principal at an elementary school told me that every school "should have a good quota of men," and that men should be given extra "stipends" as an incentive to join the teaching profession. He said, "They might have to assume more responsibilities, but certainly, any carrot that you can hang out there for them to come to [teaching] is worth looking at."

It would be difficult to institutionalize such monetary incentives to attract men to these jobs because they are located primarily in the public sector, where wages are more or less fixed. There are also laws in this country that require "equal pay for equal work."[13] Nevertheless, a substantial amount of this type of wage discrimination probably occurs and goes undetected because the preference for men in these professions is so well-entrenched among administrators.

Thus higher average salaries probably do result from increasing percentages of men. But, ultimately, recruiting men to increase professional status and pay is a disingenuous approach to solving the problems faced by predominantly female occupations. This strategy only works if employers are willing and able to pay men more than women in order to retain them. Far from eliminating the cause of these professions' lesser pay and status, this strategy reproduces it by acceding to the general cultural devaluation of women (and *over*valuation of men). Any truly transformative effort to augment the social and economic appeal of these professions would have to involve a reassessment of women's worth by society at large and a recognition of men's and women's equal claims to a living wage.

In summary, those in this study who advocated more men entering these professions articulated three sets of reasons. Some men felt that they would be less lonely and their workplaces would be more friendly and congenial if they had more male colleagues. Others maintained that employing more men in these professions would advance the social good in some way, either by dismantling gender stereotypes or by enhancing the delivery of service to the community through men's contribution of their special skills and aptitudes. Finally, some argued that more men should be recruited in order to enhance the prestige and pay of their professions.

Many respondents drew upon gender stereotypes to justify their desire for more male colleagues. Only a few individuals maintained that increasing numbers of men would (or should) undermine gender difference and inequality. The need for more men was framed by beliefs that men are essentially different from, if not better than, women: Men are needed because they are more technical, physical, or demanding than women, or else because they command higher prestige and pay than women. (Even those who did not advocate recruiting and hiring more men sometimes framed their reasons within the context of gender inequality, arguing that no more men were needed because they already monopolized the best jobs.) Far from challenging gender inequality, these reasons for wanting more men in these occupations further entrench male superiority. If men are accepted on traditionally "masculine" terms, it is likely that they will reproduce gender hierarchies within these professions.

Attracting More Men To Traditionally Female Professions

The essentially conservative implications of the kind of integration delineated above become clear from the discussions of strategies for attracting more men into these professions. Respondents attributed the underrepresentation of men in their professions to two main factors: the feminine identification of the professions, and the low pay and prestige associated with them. Depending on which reason they emphasized, they suggested different strategies for attracting more men, not all of which challenged the gender status hierarchy.

A "Woman's Job"

"It's definitely not a thing that you would do if you felt a need to have a macho image." This comment from a Texas teacher sums up the feelings of several of those interviewed about why there are so few men in their professions. Many maintained that men simply do not consider entering these fields because of their close association with "women's work." According to a California social worker:

> I have a hunch that there's not more men in the social work profession in America for the same reason there's not that many men teaching grammar school. It's considered the opposite of Rambo. It's considered feminine, and some men do not care to be considered less than a masculine person.

And when asked why more men were not employed in nursing, a former nurse now enrolled in a social work program said,

It's been handed down from generations that men are supposed to do, you know, rugged work. Go out and lay bricks and drive tractor trailers. And nursing and social work are female fields. Femininity is involved. And men aren't supposed to show emotion.

There was a virtual consensus among the respondents that the feminine identification of these professions acts as a formidable barrier to many men. However, many thought this was a false stereotype. I asked the nurse quoted above, for example, if it were true that men in nursing have more feminine attributes and more nurturing personalities than most men. He laughed heartily and said,

No! I've known other men to work in the field. In the hospital up in Minnesota there was this other man. He was a fourth degree black belt in Tai Kwan Do, but he was a nurse. And he and I had a lot in common—I like fishing, he likes fishing, and the whole nine yards. . . . So it just so happens that these are the fields that people have said that "this is masculine and this is feminine."

From his point of view, the definition of nursing as "feminine" is inaccurate, and has very little bearing on what nurses really do. His perspective was seconded by a nurse in Texas:

Because it is female-dominated, maybe men have trouble with that. . . . [But] the women you work with are really smart. . . . There's a lot of technical stuff that goes into nursing. You see how much the doctors don't know, and realize how much the nurses do. That's a scary thought. Especially when you're by yourself, you realize how much people are dependent on you. If you just say, "I don't know the answer," well, you better find out the answer, because somebody's going to die.

This man believed that the stereotype that nurses are "stupid airheads" was false, but it probably keeps men out of the profession.

Other respondents emphasized the physical or technical aspects of their work to dispute the stereotype that femininity is required for professional success. A California librarian said,

I find that a lot of people, their concept of a library is not valid. When I say I work in a library, they figure I sit and read all day. Which I don't. We're much more physically active than people think, and there's much more diversity than people think.

A female librarian agreed that the stereotypes about her profession are misleading and probably scare off potential male recruits:

I think the local communities and society at large don't perceive what I really see are the complexities of the profession nowadays, particularly in the technical, computer-oriented perspective. And so I think there's going to have to be a change in that image before men would be attracted to it.

If the feminine stereotypes about these professions are simply false, then attracting more men to them becomes an "image problem," solved with better publicity. Thus, a children's librarian claimed that more men would enter the profession "if people talked about it more . . . which nobody did for me." He said,

> As many years that I spent going into libraries, it
> never occurred to me as a profession until literally I
> just fell on top of it. Within a year of doing it, I
> thought, "Wow, people make money doing this!"

Increasing the visibility of appropriately masculine men
in popular media portrayals of these professions was often cited as a necessary first step in challenging the inaccurate "feminine" stereotypes.

Other respondents, however, were less willing to reject
as false the feminine identification of their professions.
They thought that men with extremely masculine personalities would not be suited to work in these fields. For
example, a teacher suggested that most men might not
be "patient" enough to work around children; another
thought that, in general, men were "repelled by younger
children." A librarian said that success in his profession
required "a personal quality of being willing to let the ego
step back a minute and serve somebody else, trying to
meet their needs rather than being in a position of im-
posing your needs upon them." He felt that these qualities
are lacking in most men, in contrast to women, who are
"brought up to serve." And a social worker who claimed
that men avoided his profession because "it's not a very
masculine kind of thing to do," elaborated:

> If you're a man who needs to . . . the only way you
> can feel gratified, you know, to feed your ego, is to
> be in the kind of position that you're above every-
> body else, in command, and all that shit, I should
> think that you wouldn't want to be a social worker.

Those who felt that there was a mismatch between the
masculine personality and the demands of their professions argued that attracting more men would require a
masculinizing of their work, or a feminizing of men. That

is, either the professions would have to emphasize their technical, administrative, or physical components to attract more men, or men would have to be encouraged to develop more nurturing, service-oriented personalities. Some respondents advocated both of these strategies. For example, a children's librarian first defended the former strategy of masculinizing the work:

> The traditional males just don't see themselves as earning their livelihood and reinforcing their masculinity by helping. They're not there to help. You know, they're supposed to know everything already, right? You know, you have your assistants help, but you're the one that's authoritative and you know what's what and all this sort of a thing. Maybe in a sense, if that somehow can change [more men will enter the profession]. Maybe emphasizing more of the information aspect of the profession. Sort of instilling this sense of expertise and that sort of thing.

Later he suggested that increasing the number of men in his field would require men to change their value orientation to be more like women's:

> Let's just say there are more men in some of these nontraditional professions, and they're choosing them because maybe they don't want to live up to some of these stereotypes we were talking about. Maybe they figure, "I don't want any part of the rat race. Let some other bozo do that. I want to raise a family, and I want to enjoy life. There's more to life than just working." . . . I think every year there will be more and more of those men deciding that, and, hopefully, with luck, some of them were raised that way as little boys.

I agree that the feminine identification of these professions is a major factor inhibiting men from considering careers in these areas. Making these occupations seem more "masculine," or changing men to make them more "feminine" probably would help to increase the number of men in these professions. If the ultimate goal of integration is to promote gender equality, however, both of these strategies are problematic. Emphasizing the "masculine" qualities needed in these jobs—such as technical proficiency and physical power—would probably entrench the advantages that men already have. If occupations further institutionalized these qualities by making them requirements for hiring and promotion, this would no doubt contribute to the "glass escalator," and reproduce gender hierarchies within these professions. Women in these professions would be faced with the options of either conforming to these new male standards, or fighting a rearguard battle to preserve the nurturing and otherwise more "feminine" elements of their professions.[14]

Note that this strategy is rarely—if ever—discussed as a means to increase women's representation in predominantly male fields. I have never heard policymakers suggest emphasizing the more caring, "feminine" elements of the medical, legal, or engineering professions to make them more appealing to female recruits. At issue, of course, is the general cultural devaluation of "the feminine," which those advocating the "masculinization" of these professions do little to challenge.

The alternative strategy—feminizing men—seems much less problematic, at least on the surface. Women have for years been told that to improve their economic and social status they ought to become more "like men." Books about professional and corporate careers offer plenty of advice to women about succeeding in a "man's world" by playing by the rules of their games. Rarely does anyone suggest that men ought to learn to play by *wom-*

en's rules. It seems reasonable to encourage men to become more "like women," and teach them to value those qualities and characteristics typically associated with women. If this would happen—and it is by no means certain that it will happen—more men might be attracted to the "women's professions."

But the danger here, too, is that gender hierarchy will be reproduced. When men perform tasks typically carried out by women, it is not uncommon that they are singled out for attention and praise. Even a man who cares for his own children, or regularly cooks his family's meals is often the subject of admiration, particularly from women who appreciate the effort and sacrifice involved in doing this work. Caregiving and nurturing are considered natural attributes in a woman but exceptional skills in a man. So if men entered the "women's professions" demonstrating the same character traits and skills typically attributed to women, they might still garner more recognition and rewards. "Feminizing men" therefore should be endorsed only if it is accompanied by a recognition that attributes currently associated with women are valuable and complex skills—no matter who possesses them.

A "Woman's Wage"

According to the respondents, relatively low pay is the second major reason why men are underrepresented in these jobs. In fact, even though men who work in these fields earn on average more money than their female colleagues, they earn less money than men working in comparable occupations that are predominantly male.[15]

Some respondents claimed that women were to blame for the low salaries of their occupations. A social worker in private practice lamented:

If the profession can get up to and maintain a level of professionalism with salaries around $60–80,000 a year, then men will enter it. The difficulty for me and guys like me is . . . we have trouble getting our female colleagues to charge enough. . . . They are just kind of struggling along wondering if it's okay if they charge $40 an hour.

Others blamed society and the general devaluation of women and women's work for the low pay of their professions. One man was adamant that lower salaries in social work resulted from the sexist biases of powerful men:

It's because of the males that [social work] is so low paid! It's males. I'm a victim of being a member of a female-dominated profession. I have men to blame for the predicament I'm in, not women. They're the power brokers. They've funded all the programs out here. Who's sitting in Congress? A bunch of millionaire men, and a few token women. . . . They don't value [social work].

Regardless of who is blamed for their lower salaries, several respondents maintained that the limited earning potential of these occupations is a major disincentive to men. Because men have so many options for better paying jobs, they argued, many men do not even consider entering these occupations. A school librarian told me, "Men who become teachers either don't stay long (unless they're in coaching and getting an extra stipend), or they don't go into it in the first place because IBM offers them more money." This view was shared by a social worker:

There are so many opportunities out there for males. I mean, males dominate. If you can make a lot of money doing [a certain job], then males dominate that profession. So that might be a big consideration [for men]. You've got somebody thinking, "M.S.W.? or M.B.A.? That was an easy decision to make!" Maybe I'm exaggerating, but I think that.

And a librarian claimed that so few men entered the library profession because "with the same ambition and intelligence, you could go to work in a bank and make a lot more."

Some men and women said that they had difficulty supporting themselves on their incomes. For example, a Texas teacher who argued that men avoid teaching "because there is no pay," described his financial situation:

I started at $13,000 a year [in 1981]. For a month I thought I was rich and then I realized I was going to have peanut butter sandwiches and macaroni all the time. . . . And the only way to have your standard of living go up is to go into administration. . . . If my wife and I want to have children, if we want to continue to work on our house and have children and go on vacations, one of us—she's an educator, too— one of us would probably have to go into administration someday.

He believed, along with several others, that beginning salaries are not the problem; rather, they complained that there is "no place to go" in their occupations. That is, there are no career advancement opportunities aside from entering administrative positions. They maintained that men are often forced to leave these occupations if they want to earn reasonable incomes.[16] Several suggested that to recruit and retain men, career ladders ought to be introduced, which would reward achievement and tenure with higher salaries.

Many respondents—both men and women—believed

that the salary issue is especially pressing for men due to their expectation of fulfilling a "breadwinner" role in their families. One Texas teacher explained,

You can't have a family and be a one-earner family on a teacher's salary. So that's another thing guys have to consider, you know. If they want a family, they're going to have a family where their wife works, too, or accept a very, very low, middle-class existence that has no frills whatsoever. And I can't think of very many college graduates who would accept that, as a condition of employment, that your wife is going to have to work, too.

A social worker concurred:

I think that a lot of men are still socialized, perhaps rightly, that their role is the breadwinner, and so forth. And social work is not traditionally an astonishingly high paying field. So some men who see themselves as having to fulfill that role almost exclusively—perhaps without the financial participation of the female partner—might decide to opt out of social work, even if that's where their interests were, for fear that they could not be the breadwinner.

Being unable to live up to the breadwinner role was deeply frustrating to some, illustrated most poignantly by this Massachusetts teacher:

I do feel severe financial pressure, and that has to do entirely with the notion of the role of males in society. It has nothing else to do with but that. I'm married, and my wife is earning $12,000 more than I am. . . . And although she's very supportive of me being a teacher, it's clear that she's not used to being in a role where she's the primary breadwinner. We want to have a family. She didn't consider . . . having a baby and then going back to work immediately. But we're forced to consider basically that alternative because of my income. . . . I'm the one who's not living up to . . . [my] role as the primary breadwinner. I feel that pressure intensely, and on some days, it can really destroy my sense of self-esteem to the point of wanting to rage against the world for not paying me for what I do.

This man is not economically deprived; his joint family income is approximately $70,000 per year. Rather, he is angry because his salary alone is not adequate to support his family at a middle-class standard of living. He sees this as his responsibility—and even his entitlement—as a man.

Some men frankly admitted that they felt emasculated if their incomes were not higher than their wives' incomes. A librarian lamented that "my wife was earning more than I was for a number of years; now we're kind of even. But that was not always easy." A teacher described a similar experience:

I don't feel like I'm providing adequately for my family. . . . My wife's a teacher also, a music teacher. And several points along the way, she has made more money than I have. And that doesn't set well with a male ego. The "provider" image, that I'm supposed to provide for my family, is many times absent. Again, that's another deterrent for males going into elementary education, or staying in the classroom.

Only a few men claimed that pay was not an issue keeping men as a whole out of these occupations. These men compared their incomes to working-class salaries, or nonprofessional jobs in the civil service. For example, a social worker in Arizona said,

I'm making just as much as someone working in a factory or anywhere else. . . . But there was a time when I first got in it, that I would look at it and ask myself, "Is this really what I want to do?" because of my financial obligations. But what I found out is that I liked what I was doing. I can make the money. I may not have as much as Joe Blow working in the factory, but I found out that if I was conservative and thrifty, I could have just as much as he got.

Although he maintained that salary was not a factor keeping men out of his profession, this respondent was unique in comparing his salary to that earned by men in factory jobs, instead of comparing it to the salaries of men in male-dominated professions. Working-class men may be overrepresented among the men in these occupations, which do pay better than many of the alternatives available to them. In contrast, those who compare their potential incomes with law or medicine probably find these female occupations gravely lacking in remuneration.

Gay men may also be overrepresented in these occupations in part because of the salary issue. Gay men may be more open than heterosexual men are to earning "a woman's wage," and combining it with the wages of others to sustain a middle-class standard of living. Due to their alternative family arrangements, they may be less committed to maintaining the male breadwinner role.[17]

For straight men, the social and psychological issues at stake in earning a "woman's wage" can outweigh purely economic factors. A social worker who said his profession does not "pay enough" to attract men, described his own indecision about entering the profession:

It wasn't so much that it didn't pay enough for me to live a reasonably comfortable life. It was that it didn't pay enough for me to maintain my masculine image.

He said that to attract large numbers of men to predominantly female occupations, salaries would have to be exceptionally high to compensate them for this "emasculation":

> I know that there are men who go into nursing, but the men who I've talked to who've gone into nursing have gone into nursing because the salaries are so good, and they were willing to deal with the discomfort of being out of role, out of the gender role. But you can't say that about social work.

Would higher pay attract more men into these occupations? This is a difficult question to answer, as there is very little historical precedent. Very few female occupations have ever become gender-balanced; even fewer have changed entirely from female-to-male (in contrast to many that have changed from male-to-female). Among those that have changed are spinning and other textile manufacture, and midwifery. In both cases, the entry of large numbers of men into these occupations was precipitated by substantial technological transformations of the work, and a redefinition of the activity as appropriate only for men. The perception of enhanced economic opportunities may have drawn some men into these fields, but not until the new technology was defined as appropriately masculine did men enter in great numbers.[18]

Likewise, today, there is very little indication that men are becoming more interested in predominantly female occupations, despite some improvement in their salaries. In some urban areas, for example, salaries for nurses improved during the 1980s due to a perceived nursing shortage, but men did not flock to the occupation as a consequence (although their numbers have increased). Such an "invasion" of men would probably first require a redefinition of the occupation as suitably masculine.

Throughout U.S. history, the promise of a good salary has not drawn large numbers of men into predominantly female occupations. Even devastating economic hardship has failed to attract men to women's jobs: The degree of sex segregation of occupations remains relatively stable in periods of recession, and men and women have similar rates of unemployment in both tight and slack job markets.[19] In a study of AT&T workers, Cynthia Fuchs Epstein found that some men would rather suffer unemployment than accept a relatively good "woman's wage" because it would damage their self-esteem.[20] The economic value of the wage is not the only—or perhaps even the major—impediment to men's entry into these jobs.

Although higher pay alone probably will not attract large numbers of men into these occupations, I do believe that instituting "career ladders" would help retain the men already working in these jobs. But I do not endorse this strategy, because in all likelihood, career ladders will reproduce the "glass escalator" and do little to enhance women's status in these occupations. Typically, career ladders reward those who conform to a male career pattern of early education, long periods of uninterrupted tenure, and workdays free of any distractions from family life. Instituting career ladders therefore would probably enhance men's status in predominantly female occupations, unless the criteria for promotion were devised specifically according to the work patterns more typical of women's careers.

In sum, the various strategies recommended to increase the proportion of men in these professions would probably work to a greater or lesser extent. But if implemented, they would not necessarily contribute to the diminishment of gender inequality. Making these professions more "masculine" or instituting career ladders to attract more men would reproduce gender hierarchies. In the former case, qualities associated with men would be sought after and rewarded; in the latter case, men's typical career patterns would probably continue to be used as the standards for success. If the goal of breaking down segregation is to lessen women's oppression—not further entrench male privilege—then these strategies should not be pursued.

Any effort to hire more men in these predominantly female occupations must consider the potential effects on women workers. Women workers must be guaranteed rights to the same opportunities and advantages that men already have by virtue of our sexist culture, which values men and qualities associated with masculinity more highly than women and female-identified qualities. Recognizing women's right to successful and rewarding careers would require a radical reassessment of the low value placed on women. Without such a reappraisal of women's worth, men's entry into traditionally female occupations will, in all likelihood, further entrench gender inequality.

Conclusion

Occupational sex segregation is a major problem for working women. It contributes to the income gap between men and women; it perpetuates gender stereotypes; and it impedes women from pursuing some of the most powerful and fulfilling careers in our society. But lessening segregation by intentionally integrating the "women's professions" will not necessarily help to eliminate gender inequality. Because our society values men more highly than women, there is always a danger that men will displace women workers, or take over the best jobs. Any effort to recruit more men into these fields, therefore, must carefully consider the consequences for women workers, and take steps to protect their interests.

The men who currently work in predominantly female professions occupy an extremely contradictory position in terms of the gender order of our society. On the one hand, they are the "pioneers" on the forefront of integration. Unlike the vast majority of men, most of the men in these professions work closely with women as colleagues, and they engage in activities that society has labeled "feminine." The male kindergarten teacher, school librarian, nurse, or caseworker represents an enormous potential challenge to our assumptions about men's natural proclivities and their "proper place" in society.

Yet, even as these men represent a potential challenge to the gender system, they also have a stake in that system. Because of the higher value placed on men by the larger society, men extract advantages within these occupations. Men enter these professions carrying their gender privilege with them, and consequently they "rise to the top," outearning their female colleagues and reproducing the same gender hierarchies that characterize other professions.

This contradictory position of these men—as both challengers to the gender system, and beneficiaries of that system—makes the issue of occupational integration much more complex in these professions than in other, male-dominated professions. When women enter all-male enclaves, they do not bring any special privileges or advantages with them. Instead, their gender is a source of scorn and derision, so many women try to downplay their difference from men in order to escape negative re-percussions.[21] Women need policies such as affirmative action and "targeted" recruitment drives to "level the playing field" and compensate them for the additional ob-stacles they must overcome in order to enter and succeed in these jobs.

The evidence presented here suggests that men do not face this kind of barrier in predominantly female jobs. Even in these contexts, men are privileged over women; affirmative action type policies designed for men are not needed. If anything, women continue to need the benefit of such special consideration even in these predomi-nantly female fields—especially for top positions, where they are underrepresented.

But excluding men from these jobs is not the right so-lution. I believe that men should be encouraged to enter these professions—but only on the same terms as women. Nursing, teaching, social work, and librarianship need caring and dedicated people, and it would be a positive social change if men were encouraged to develop these "feminine" skills and orientations. But clearly, recruiting men for their "special" proclivities or powers will simply reproduce the gender status hierarchy within these pro-fessions and do nothing to improve the lot of women working in these jobs. The ultimate goal of gender equal-ity should frame all efforts at integration. Otherwise, the radical potential of "men doing women's work" will be lost.

The U.S. feminist movement has encouraged women to enter "male" fields, and it has promoted policies in-tended to make women more competitive with men in these jobs. This is an important and essential step on the road to gender equality; opening up men's jobs to wom-en gives women the opportunity to achieve economic independence from men, and helps to break down limiting stereotypes about women's capabilities. But well-meaning efforts directed at getting women to be more "like men" run the risk of reifying the male standard, making men the ultimate measure of success. If the aim is gender equality, then men should be encouraged to become more "like women" by developing, or feeling free to express, interests and skills in traditionally feminine activities, and crossing over to predominantly female jobs.

It is almost overwhelming to imagine the preconditions for men becoming "like women" on a large scale as this would require a radical transformation of society and the male psyche. As a group, men would somehow have to learn to respect, value, and identify with women—an ideal that seems extremely elusive in the current climate of social backlash against women and feminism. Men who have reassessed masculinity and are working to radically transform it are often the subject of ridicule and scorn (not unlike the men in this study who "cross over" to the other side). But short of promoting separatism, transforming men is the only logical solution to the problem of gender inequality. Women have been working for decades to become men's equals. It is now time for men to work at becoming women's equals.

8

Conclusion

The sociology of occupations has been conducted for the
most part with gender-neutral frameworks. Most conventional organizational theory ignores gender, except as an
extraneous variable that is either irrelevant or disruptive
to smooth bureaucratic functioning.[1] In this book, I have
argued that occupations are deeply gendered. Organizations do not simply create slots, indifferent to what kind
of worker fills what positions. Jobs are created for men
or for women; assumptions about the gender of the
worker are embedded in job descriptions, hierarchies,
and workplace practices. Moreover, workers do not check
their gender at the office door or the factory gates. Individuals bring gendered interests and desires to their jobs.
For over a century, work has been one of the most important arenas for the consolidation and reproduction of
gender identity—particularly for men. Although not all
men achieve success in the work world, as Acker points
out, "masculinity always seems to symbolize self-respect

for men at the bottom and power for men at the top, while confirming for both their gender's superiority."[2]

Even in predominantly female occupations, masculinity is continually created and reproduced. Chapter 2 describes how expectations about the gender of the worker became embedded in nursing, teaching, librarianship, and social work. From the nineteenth century on, job descriptions and hierarchies assumed that women would perform most of the work in these occupations, but that men would manage and administer their workplace organizations. However, these assumptions were not set permanently; the gendered structuring of organizations is constantly in flux and open to negotiation. The twentieth-century drive for "professionalization" represented a struggle over these gendered assumptions. The leadership in these occupations recruited men and encouraged women to develop more masculine orientations to their work as explicit strategies to enhance occupational pay and prestige. This history illustrates the dynamic interplay between the interests and needs of individuals (what Simmel called the "contents" of social interaction), and the forms that are institutionalized in social structure.[3]

This dynamic interplay is demonstrated today in men's experiences in these predominantly female occupations. There is still a widespread popular assumption that the men in these occupations are "anomalies" because they work in "female" jobs. But the men who enter these careers do not, for the most part, conceive of themselves in this way (see chapter 3). They are typically drawn into these occupations through their experiences in more conventional jobs, and they are encouraged by close friends and family members who reassure them that their masculinity will not be questioned by making such a move.

Indeed, many men had no idea just how nontraditional their new careers were until they entered professional school, where there were only a handful of other men in their classes.

Being a token results in some predictable patterns of interaction. Like all tokens, these men stand out more than their peers, and receive more than their fair share of attention. There is also evidence of "boundary heightening" when men are tokens: Differences between males and females are highlighted in very stereotypical ways. Yet these effects of tokenism are not always negative for men (see chapter 4). Because qualities associated with masculinity are more highly regarded than qualities associated with femininity—even within the predominantly female culture of these professional schools—men tend to excel in these contexts. Moreover, men actively participate in this boundary heightening. When the two male nursing students wore golfing caps to their graduation, they drew attention to their lack of conformity with the dominant group. But far from being ostracized for this difference, they were applauded: One of the two was, after all, class president.

The theory of tokenism predicts that *all* numerical minorities will suffer negative job consequences.[4] But men's experiences in predominantly female occupations show this is simply not the case. Because men and the qualities associated with masculinity are highly valued by organizations, any difference from women is actively sought after and reproduced by token men as a source of advantage and prestige.

The advantages that accrue to token men in organizations are especially clear in the workplace. I have argued that nursing, teaching, librarianship, and social work are biased in favor of men. The top positions in these fields—

like those in most bureaucratic organizations—draw upon and reproduce so-called masculine characteristics. The library director or welfare administrator is expected to be career-driven, aggressive, decisive, and rational—precisely those traits believed to be more prevalent in men than women. And even when men work alongside women in "feminine" specialties, their contributions are differentiated from women's in ways that benefit men. Supervisors and co-workers often expect men to be more driven and competent than women (see chapter 5). Men do occasionally encounter negative reactions from the public: If they work mostly around children, for example, they are sometimes suspected of being sexually "perverted." Ironically, these negative stereotypes can add to the pressure men face to "move up" in their professions to specialties considered more legitimate for men.

These occupations treat men and women differently, and men, generally benefiting as a result, are not passive in this process of differentiation (see chapter 6). They actively redefine their work, and cast their participation in these jobs as consistent with hegemonic masculinity.

Precisely what it means to be masculine constantly changes, reflecting the dynamic interplay between the organizational structure of the occupation and the needs and desires brought to the workplace by individual men. However, I have argued that masculinity is *always* defined in terms of its "opposite": femininity. In other words, to be masculine always means to be different from and better than women. What this involves will vary from context to context. In general, it means occupying a position of power over women and other men, or making a higher salary than women. But for the male children's librarian, being masculine might mean being "physical" during story hour, and for the male nurse, it might mean catheterizing a male patient. These are activities that women engage in every day, but they are appropriated and used by the men as evidence—however tenuous—that they are masculine.

Much is at stake in men's efforts to secure a masculine gender identity. Proving themselves as different from and better than women positions them to excel within these jobs and advance up the job hierarchy. Because masculine qualities are sought out for the top jobs, men entering these professions today are often whisked to the top very early in their careers. This process is facilitated by the men (and sometimes the women) occupying the highest rungs in these professions, who can and do make hiring and promotion decisions that favor men. Organizations are fundamentally male insofar as they value masculine qualities more highly than feminine ones. Men who successfully present themselves as suitably masculine thus stand to benefit in very tangible ways.

I have argued that, *in addition to* these material benefits, men may experience a psychological incentive to engage in this reproduction of masculinity. According to psychoanalytic theory, many men desire to differentiate from and subordinate women because of traumatic conflicts experienced during childhood. Early in life, boys raised in traditional nuclear families are typically forced to forgo their original feminine identification in favor of a masculine one—a traumatic experience because it requires them to give up an intimate and emotionally intense attachment to their mothers. Moreover, this transition is very difficult for many boys because they rarely come into intimate daily contact with adult men. Boys who lack "real life" male role models tend to define masculinity negatively, as whatever is not feminine, which means denying and repressing any association with women.[5]

A central premise in psychoanalytic theory is that early conflicts and traumatic experiences are rarely resolved completely. Instead, they become lodged in the unconscious, periodically resurfacing throughout adult life. Thus, early childhood conflicts experienced over the acquisition of a masculine identity could be reasserting themselves in adult men's desire to establish difference and superiority over women. Heightening gender differences at work may in part be a response to these unconscious psychological desires.[6]

Because there is both a structural and a psychological component to the reproduction of gender differences at work, any effort to achieve gender parity at work must address *both* sources of differentiation (see chapter 7). That is, for men and women to be truly equal at work, the organizational arrangements that privilege men must be transformed, and the psychological incentives that impel individual men to strive for differentiation from women must also change.

Although the case studies in this book represent extremes of gender segregation, the organizational processes governing the treatment of men and women in them are characteristic of other occupations as well. Occupational segregation by gender is extreme in this country, and its consequences are seen in the persistent gap between men's and women's incomes. The changes I advocate for the "women's professions" must be applied to the job market in general in order to achieve economic equality for women. In my view, all organizations must be restructured to place equal value on so-called masculine and feminine characteristics. There is no compelling instrumental reason why emotional expressiveness and empathy are devalued by organizations. Workplaces might become more congenial and perhaps even more productive if workers were encouraged to develop these "feminine" qualities. Furthermore, workplace organizations must reassess the highly anachronistic assumption that workers have no obligations outside of work. Today this accurately describes only those conforming to the traditional breadwinner role—for the most part, a very select group of men. Organizations must be made more flexible to enable workers with integral domestic responsibilities to achieve success and recognition in their jobs. Currently, those who forgo meaningful domestic lives are rewarded for doing so, giving men an unfair advantage over women in the labor market.

Making these structural changes in the interests of achieving gender equality seems a remote possibility today. These organizational patterns reflect the interests of the powerful men who control most large-scale organizations. Breaking men's monopoly on organizational power is not likely to happen anytime soon, especially with the current backlash against social policies such as affirmative action. Perhaps even more remote is the second imperative for change; that is, the need to change men. It is my argument that the drive to differentiate from and subordinate women found in so many men today is *in part* a product of male socialization in traditional nuclear families where all responsibility for child rearing is shouldered by the mother. This configuration typically compels the boy to violently break from his feminine identification and strive for an impossibly illusive masculine ideal that denigrates the earlier tie to the mother. As long as men are socialized to desire this differentiation, I believe they will continue to creatively redefine and sustain their masculinity at the expense of women.

It is almost overwhelming to consider all it would take to change men so that they would not desire differentiation from women. The entire structure and ideology of the nuclear family would have to be transformed to enable men and women to share equally in the care of children. Achieving this goal of equal participation in childcare would require revolutionary upheavals in every other sphere of society, including workplace organizations, public policy, and cultural institutions that reproduce beliefs about femininity and masculinity.[7]

But there may be some hope on the horizon. Lynne Segal is cautiously optimistic about changing men because more men are becoming involved in child rearing, alternative masculinities are becoming more prominent, and feminists are becoming more influential in politics. Granted, she does believe that these changes are happening in "slow motion," the aptly named title of her book on changing masculinity.[8]

I think that the men who work in nontraditional occupations might also represent a ray of hope for change, but not in any straightforward way. I have argued that many of the men who do "women's work" see themselves as operating entirely within the paradigm of hegemonic masculinity. However, the next generation may be forming completely different impressions of masculinity because of them. While discussing his views about the differences between male and female teachers, a male first grade teacher alluded to this possibility:

By the end of the [school] year, most of my students call me mamma. [laughs] So that tells you that, you know, that my [male] image has disappeared. . . . It's not that I'm substituting for their mother. It's just that they're getting tired and they're forgetting who they're talking to. It's kind of flattering to know that, you know, the child trusts you that much to call you mother. I get called mamma more than I get called daddy. But that's because most of my kids don't have fathers.

If more men were intimately involved in caring for young children—as fathers or as teachers, nurses, librarians, and social workers—then boys would not have to define masculinity as the negation of femininity: They would have "real life" male role models with whom to identify. And insofar as these adult men are seen by the children as actively engaging in nurturing tasks, the boys' definition of masculinity could begin to change, and include heretofore "feminine" qualities. Thus, even though the men who do "women's work" may be *personally* committed to gender differentiation, their very presence in these occupations might cloud the distinction between mamma and daddy. This, it seems to me, is an important step toward achieving gender equality.

Methodological Appendix

This study is based on in-depth interviews with seventy-six men and twenty-three women in four occupations: nursing, elementary school teaching, librarianship, and social work. Interviews were conducted from 1985 through 1991 in four metropolitan areas. The ninety-nine people who participated in this study were selected using "snowballing" techniques. I found contacts through "word of mouth," training schools, friends of friends, and workplaces. I used the technique of "theoretical" sampling.[1] Respondents were purposively selected to capture the array of men's experiences in these occupations. Thus, I interviewed practitioners in every specialty, oversampling those employed in the *most* gender-atypical areas (e.g., male kindergarten teachers and school librarians). I also selected respondents from throughout the occupational hierarchies—from students to administrators to retirees.

Interviews were conducted in four cites: Austin, Texas; San Francisco-Oakland, California; Boston, Massachusetts; and Phoenix, Arizona. I chose different venues in order to represent regional cultural variation. However, the individuals in the study did not necessarily come from the cities where they were interviewed. There is substantial mobility within these occupations: Positions are advertised nationally, and most of the respondents had moved from a different state for their current job. Thus, one of the nurses I interviewed in Texas went to nursing school in Brooklyn; a California librarian was from

Nebraska. The teachers were the most likely to have attended school in the same state where they worked.

I chose these cities, too, because they cover a broad range in terms of the proportions of men employed in these occupations. Using 1980 Census data, I calculated the proportions of men in each of these occupations in the 150 largest U.S. metropolitan areas. In table A, I show the "rank" of each of these four cities in terms of their proportions of men for each occupation. Thus, Austin has one of the highest percentages of men in nursing, whereas Phoenix's percentage is one of the lowest. Table B shows the number of respondents interviewed in each profession in each city.

I personally conducted all of the interviews, which lasted between one and two hours. The interview questionnaire consisted of several open-ended questions on four broad topics: motivation to enter the profession; experiences in training; career progression; and general views about men's status and prospects within these occupations. Interviews took place in restaurants, my home or office, or the respondent's home or office. With only a few exceptions, interviews were tape-recorded and transcribed for this analysis.

Respondents were given consent forms detailing their rights as participants in this study. I guaranteed both anonymity and confidentiality. All proper names in the text have been changed and some quotes have been slightly altered to protect the identity of the respondents.

Interviewing men about their experiences raises questions about "sex of interviewer effects," a term survey researchers use to describe differences in how people respond to a male and a female interviewer. With Joel Heikes, who interviewed male nurses for a separate project, I investigated the impact of the researcher's gender on interview findings.[2] We found subtle differences in how our two samples of men framed their responses to our questions. When talking to the male interviewer, respondents tended to state their opinions about gender differences in a much more direct manner, typically using an "us versus them" (or "men versus women") framework. In my

Table A
Proportion of Men in Selected Occupations in Four Standard Metropolitan Statistical Areas (SMSA's), 1980

	Nursing med.[a] = 3.7		Teaching (elem.) med. = 25.0		Librarianship med. = 16.2		Social Work med. = 35.0	
	% men	rank[b]	% men	rank	% men	rank	% men	rank
Austin	7.7	140	17.3	20	21.6	116	36.1	86
Boston	3.1	47	27.5	99	20.8	109	32.0	50
S.F.-Oak.	5.6	126	26.6	86	26.7	142	37.2	100
Phoenix	2.7	37	26.7	90	14.1	56	46.1	137

SOURCE: Table calculated from U.S. Bureau of the Census, *Detailed Population Characteristics*, table 219: Detailed Occupation of Employed Persons by SMSA (Washington, D.C.: Government Printing Office, 1984). My thanks to Cynthia Chavez for her assistance in compiling this table.

[a]"Med." refers to the median proportion of men in this occupation for the 150 SMSA's included in this analysis.

[b]Rank among the largest 150 SMSA's in the U.S. (where 1 = lowest proportion men, and 150 = highest proportion men)

Table B
*Number of Respondents,
by Occupation and Location*

	Nurses	Social Workers	Librarians	Teachers	TOTAL
Ariz.	3	3	3	4	13
Calif.	15	6	7	6	34
Mass.	3	4	6	3	16
Texas	5	7	13	11	36
TOTAL	26	20	29	24	99

interviews, many men seemed reluctant to make any claims about "all women," and they tried to avoid offending my apparently feminist sensibilities.

This is called the "social desirability bias" in interviews, which is the tendency of voluntary research participants to adjust their statements so that they sound more desirable to the interviewer. Respondents will usually make assumptions about the interviewer's beliefs using gender as a "cue," and they will diplomatically figure out a way to share their own beliefs without offending the interviewer.

There were several examples of this social desirability bias in this study. When I asked a librarian if he felt either accepted or ostracized by his female colleagues, he said,

> I've never felt any resentment from any of my colleagues. I think perhaps at meetings. . . . If a meeting consists of mainly women—and there are a lot of women administrators in the library profession, it's not just men at the top—it seems to me that they will listen more. . . . Let me see, how can I put this? I don't mean to sound sexist at all. But I think because I'm a man, I get listened to more closely than if I were a woman, by women. Not necessarily by men, but by women.

In several instances, men stopped themselves in mid-sentence, and reframed their responses because they felt their views might be taken "the wrong way" by me. A special education teacher, who was describing the benefits of working in his specialty (versus regular education), said,

> A person who wants to be creative has no outlet in elementary schools, except for the stupid bulletin boards. [laughs]
>
> [CW: And special ed?]
>
> In special ed, that's the freest area of all. I think men are less likely to . . . uh . . . The procedures of elementary education—regular elementary education—are so prescribed and they're so numerous and so complex that most men just do not abide by that. It would take a real . . . I don't know, a real special man to endure all of that.

This is a good example of how respondents negotiate the gendered context of the interview. This teacher wanted to communicate to me that men are underrepresented in elementary education because they are less well-suited than women are to its conformist methods and practices. But he had to find a diplomatic way of saying that without offending or threatening the interviewer. His comments are a particularly adroit example of this speech diplomacy.

The fact that in-depth interviews allow respondents to clarify their beliefs in this diplomatic way is one of the strengths of this method. Respondents are able to communicate even hostile and sexist views without directly challenging the sensibilities of the interviewer. In contrast, studies that use a forced-choice answer format may provoke respondents to give misleading replies so as not to insult the interviewer.

But it is crucial to recognize that my gender did leave an indelible stamp on the interview data. This is not to suggest that when men conduct interviews with men the results are necessarily more "truthful" or honest. Every interview takes place in a gendered context—either the context of gender similarity or gender difference—and this context will structure the information collected. There is no archimedean point outside the gender system that allows for the collection of pure and unbiased data. But keeping in mind the efforts of men to "save face" and appear socially desirable in their remarks does help us to understand more about how gender is negotiated in daily interaction.

A final methodological note is needed on my use of psycho-analytic theory in explaining men's behavior in nontraditional occupations. Sociologists of gender have generally been hostile to this theoretical tradition, in part because the standards for empirical evidence are quite different for sociology and psy-choanalysis.[3] Like most sociological studies, this project is based on one-time interviews, not in-depth case studies gath-ered over several months (or even years) of therapeutic treat-ment in analysis. For this reason, the data of my interviews cannot be used as "proof" of the psychoanalytic approach, nor do I intend them to be construed in this way. Instead, I have argued that the men's own descriptions of their experiences are consistent with the psychoanalytic claims about masculinity and the reproduction of gender differences. Psychoanalytic the-ory offers a compelling explanation of the origin of the status difference between men and women and the intensity with which men pursue gender differentiation, issues that the alter-native approaches in sociology have failed to adequately ex-plain. But I agree that different methodologies—in particular, the in-depth case study approach—are needed to refine the the-oretical approach and capture the nuances of individual iden-tity formation.

Notes

Chapter 1

1. Allan Angoff, "The Male Librarian—An Anomaly?" *Library Journal*, February 15, 1959, p. 553.

2. *Austin-American Statesman*, January 16, 1990; response by John Kelso, January 18, 1990.

3. Some of the most important studies of women in male-dominated occupations are: Rosabeth Moss Kanter, *Men and Women of the Corporation* (New York: Basic Books, 1977); Susan Martin, *Breaking and Entering: Policewomen on Patrol* (Berkeley: University of California Press, 1980); Cynthia Fuchs Epstein, *Women in Law* (New York: Basic Books, 1981); Kay Deaux and Joseph Ullman, *Women of Steel* (New York: Praeger, 1983); Judith Hicks Stiehm, *Arms and the Enlisted Woman* (Philadelphia: Temple University Press, 1989); Jerry Jacobs, *Revolving Doors: Sex Segregation and Women's Careers* (Stanford: Stanford University Press, 1989); Barbara Reskin and Patricia Roos, *Job Queues, Gender Queues: Explaining Women's Inroads into Male Occupations* (Philadelphia: Temple University Press, 1990).

Among the few books that do examine men's status in predominantly female occupations are Carol Tropp Schreiber, *Changing Places: Men and Women in Transitional Occupations* (Cambridge: MIT Press, 1979); Christine L. Williams, *Gender Differences at Work: Women and Men in Nontraditional Occupations* (Berkeley: University of California Press, 1989); and

Christine L. Williams, ed., *Doing "Women's Work": Men in Non-traditional Occupations* (Newbury Park, CA: Sage Publications, 1993).

4. In an influential essay on methodological principles, Herbert Blumer counseled sociologists to "sedulously seek participants in the sphere of life who are acute observers and who are well informed. One such person is worth a hundred others who are merely unobservant participants." See "The Methodological Position of Symbolic Interactionism," in *Symbolic Interactionism: Perspective and Method* (Berkeley: University of California Press, 1969), p. 41.

5. The overall proportions in the population do not necessarily represent the experiences of individuals in my sample. Some nurses, for example, worked in groups that were composed almost entirely of men, while some social workers had the experience of being the only man in their group. The overall statistics provide a general guide, but relying on them exclusively can distort the actual experiences of individuals in the workplace. The statistics available for research on occupational sex segregation are not specific enough to measure internal divisions among workers. Research that uses firm-level data finds a far greater degree of segregation than research that uses national data. See William T. Bielby and James N. Baron, "A Woman's Place Is with Other Women: Sex Segregation within Organizations," in *Sex Segregation in the Workplace: Trends, Explanations, Remedies,* ed. Barbara Reskin (Washington, D.C.: National Academy Press, 1984), pp. 27–55.

6. See Methodological Appendix for details about the sample and its selection.

7. In 1992, women constituted 45.7 percent of all employed persons in the United States. See U.S. Department of Labor, Bureau of Labor Statistics, *Employment and Earnings* 40, no. 1 (January 1993): 195.

8. Status attainment theory and human capital theory are reviewed in Natalie Sokoloff, *Between Money and Love* (New York: Praeger, 1980), and Margaret Mooney Marini, "Sex Dif-

ferences in Earnings in the United States," *Annual Review of Sociology* 15 (1989): 343–80.

9. For additional critiques of classical organizational theory and its treatment of gender, see Joan Acker, "Hierarchies, Jobs, Bodies: A Theory of Gendered Organizations," *Gender & Society* 4 (June 1990): 139–58; Jeff Hearn and Wendy Parkin, *Sex at Work: The Power and Paradox of Organization Sexuality* (New York: St. Martin's Press, 1987); and Rosemary Pringle, *Secretaries Talk* (London: Verso, 1988), esp. ch. 4.

10. Barbara Reskin and Polly Phipps, "Women in Male-Dominated Professional and Managerial Occupations," in *Women Working,* ed. Ann Helton Stromberg and Shirley Harkess (Mountain View, CA: Mayfield Publishing Co., 1988), pp. 190–205.

11. Kanter, *Men and Women of the Corporation,* p. 241.

12. The clearest statement of this theory is Joan Acker, "Hierarchies, Jobs, Bodies." This perspective has been greatly influenced by the work of feminist historian Joan Scott. See her "Gender: A Useful Category for Historical Analysis," *American Historical Review* 91 (1986): 1053–75. Elaine Hall uses this perspective in her study of waitresses and waiters, "Smiling, Deferring, and Flirting: Doing Gender by Giving 'Good Service,'" *Work and Occupations* 20 (1993): 452–71.

13. Acker, "Hierarchies, Jobs, Bodies," p. 149.

14. For a discussion of the unequal division of household labor, see Arlie Hochschild with Ann Machung, *The Second Shift* (New York: Avon Books, 1989).

15. A greater variety of jobs are designated for men than for women. Nearly a quarter of all working women are employed in nursing, clerical work, and waitressing. Francine D. Blau and Anne E. Winkler, "Women in the Labor Force: An Overview," in *Women: A Feminist Perspective,* ed. Jo Freeman, 4th ed. (Mountain View, CA: Mayfield Publishing Co., 1989); Marini, "Sex Differences in Earnings in the United States."

16. Reskin and Roos, *Job Queues, Gender Queues,* ch. 1.

17. U.S. Department of Labor, p. 231.

18. Nursing is somewhat of an exception in that supervisory positions were originally designated for women. However, within hospital organizations, the occupation of nursing was consciously placed under the direct supervision of physicians, an occupation which was clearly designated male-only during the nineteenth century.

19. This sort of discrimination is illegal. Title VII of the Civil Rights Act prohibits discrimination in hiring on the basis of sex, and men have won court cases against institutions that have such explicit policies. Nevertheless, these policies remain in place in various schools and hospitals, according to several of those interviewed. They may not be written policies, but they are well known and informally communicated to prospective job applicants.

20. Liliane Floge and D. M. Merrill, "Tokenism Reconsidered: Male Nurses and Female Physicians in a Hospital Setting," *Social Forces* 64 (1986): 925–47.

21. Hearn and Parkin, *Sex at Work*. For an analysis of how these images affect secretaries, see Pringle, *Secretaries Talk*.

22. For a discussion of how masculine expectations are embedded in employee evaluations in the military, see Williams, *Gender Differences at Work*, pp. 68–69.

23. See, for example, Cynthia Cockburn, *In the Way of Women* (New York: ILR Press, 1991), ch. 5.

24. Cynthia Cockburn, "The Gendering of Jobs: Workplace Relations and the Reproduction of Sex Segregation," in *Gender Segregation at Work*, ed. Sylvia Walby (Philadelphia: Open University Press, 1988), p. 38.

25. Alice Kessler-Harris, *A Woman's Wage: Historical Meanings and Social Consequences* (Lexington: University of Kentucky Press, 1990), p. 125.

26. Ava Baron, "Gender and Labor History: Learning from the Past, Looking to the Future," in *Work Engendered: Toward a New History of American Labor*, ed. Ava Baron (Ithaca, NY: Cornell University Press, 1991), pp. 1–46; Heidi Hartmann, "Capitalism, Patriarchy, and Job Segregation by Sex," in *Capitalist Patriarchy and the Case for Socialist Feminism*, ed. Zillah

Eisenstein (New York: Monthly Review Press, 1979), pp. 206–47; E. Anthony Rotundo, *American Manhood: Transformations in Masculinity from the Revolution to the Modern Era* (New York: Basic Books, 1993), esp. ch. 8.

27. Baron, "Gender and Labor History," pp. 27–32.

28. For a historical discussion of this asymmetry, see Harriet Bradley, "Across the Great Divide: The Entry of Men into Women's Jobs," in *Doing "Women's Work,"* pp. 10–27; and for a discussion of the current asymmetry, see Jerry A. Jacobs, "Men in Female-Dominated Fields: Trends and Turnover," in *Doing "Women's Work,"* pp. 49–63.

29. For an explicit comparison of men's and women's experiences in nontraditional occupations, see Williams, *Gender Differences at Work.* Robin Leidner finds additional support for this view in her analysis of fast food restaurants and the insurance industry. See *Fast Food, Fast Talk* (Berkeley: University of California Press, 1993), esp. ch. 6.

30. David H. J. Morgan, *Discovering Men* (London and New York: Routledge, 1992), p. 97.

31. This perspective is somewhat unique in the sociology of gender, especially in the United States. Sociologists' explanations of human social behavior typically emphasize social structure instead of individual agency. Perhaps this is a consequence of the historical origins of sociology, and the insistence of the discipline's founders that all social facts be explained entirely by other social facts, a position articulated most forcefully by Emile Durkheim. In this book, I attempt to combine both levels of analysis because, in my view, a complete picture of men's status and prospects in nontraditional occupations depends on a thorough understanding of both organizational structure and individual agency, and the complex interplay between them.

Chapter 2

1. Linda K. Kerber, *Women of the Republic: Intellect and Ideology in Revolutionary America* (New York: Norton, 1986), p. 59.

2. Ibid., p. 190.

3. Ruth Schwartz Cowan, *More Work for Mother* (New York: Basic Books, 1983); Maxine Margolis, *Mothers and Such* (Berkeley: University of California Press, 1984).

4. Joan J. Brumberg and Nancy Tomes, "Women in the Professions: A Research Agenda for American Historians," *Reviews in American History* 10 (June 1982): 275–96.

5. David Tyack and Myra Strober, "Jobs and Gender: A History of the Structuring of Educational Employment by Sex," in *Educational Policy and Management*, ed. Patricia Schmuck, W. W. Charters, and Richard O. Carlson (New York: Academic Press, 1981), pp. 131–52.

6. Horace Mann, *Eighth Annual Report of the Board of Education*, reprinted in W. Elliot Brownlee and Mary M. Brownlee, *Women in the American Economy* (New Haven: Yale University Press, 1976), p. 268.

7. Kathryn Kish Sklar, *Catharine Beecher: A Study in American Domesticity* (New Haven: Yale University Press, 1973), p. 97. Kindergarten teaching, unlike other types of teaching, began as a female occupation. Kindergartens were first instituted in the mid-nineteenth century by charitable organizations; they did not become part of the public school system until the first decades of the twentieth century. See Barbara Beatty, " 'A Vocation from on High': Kindergartning as an Occupation for American Women," in *Changing Education: Women as Radicals and Conservators*, ed. Joyce Antler and Sari Knopp Biklin (Albany: State University of New York Press, 1990), pp. 35–50.

8. Quoted in Sheila Rothman, *Women's Proper Place* (New York: Basic Books, 1978), p. 57.

9. Florence Nightingale, *Notes on Nursing* (1860; reprint, New York: Dover, 1969), p. 3.

10. Susan Reverby, *Ordered to Care: The Dilemma of American Nursing, 1850–1945* (Cambridge: Cambridge University Press, 1987), p. 49.

11. Margaret L. Rogers, "Private Nursing," *American Journal of Nursing* 2 (1901), p. 82.

12. Dee Garrison, *Apostles of Culture: The Public Librarian*

and American Society, 1876–1920 (New York: The Free Press, 1979), pp. 198–200; Julia Raunch, "Women in Social Work: Friendly Visitors in Philadelphia, 1880," *Social Service Review* 49 (1975): 241–59; Paula Dressel, "Patriarchy and Social Welfare Work," *Social Problems* 34 (June 1987): 294–309.

13. Mary Ryan, *Womanhood in America*, 2d ed. (New York: New Viewpoints, 1978), p. 136.

14. Penina Migdal Glazer and Miriam Slater, *Unequal Colleagues: The Entrance of Women into the Professions, 1890–1940* (New Brunswick, NJ: Rutgers University Press, 1987), p. 201.

15. Quoted in Dee Garrison, "The Tender Technicians: The Feminization of Public Librarianship, 1876–1905," *Journal of Social History* 6 (1972–73): 136.

16. *The International Congress of Women in 1899: Women in the Professions*, excerpted in *The Role of Women in Librarianship, 1876–1976*, ed. Kathleen Weibel and Kathleen M. Heim (Phoenix, AZ: Oryx Press, 1979), p. 34.

17. Garrison, *Apostles of Culture*, pp. 179–80.

18. Redding S. Sugg, *Motherteacher: The Feminization of American Education* (Charlottesville: University Press of Virginia, 1978), p. 39; Florence Nightingale, quoted in Susan Reverby, *Ordered to Care*, p. 22; Garrison, *Apostles of Culture*, p. 194. On the image of nursing, see Martha Vicinus, *Independent Women: Work and Community for Single Women, 1850–1920* (Chicago: University of Chicago Press, 1985), p. 87.

19. In many cases, women from rural areas were sent to training schools away from home, possibly exacerbating parents' fears about the propriety of these occupations. See Brumberg and Tomes, "Women in the Professions."

20. Roy Lubove, *The Professional Altruist: The Emergence of Social Work as a Career, 1880–1930* (New York: Atheneum, 1975).

21. Darlene Clark Hine, *Black Women in White: Racial Conflict and Cooperation in the Nursing Profession, 1890–1950* (Bloomington: Indiana University Press, 1989), p. 6.

22. Lubove, *The Professional Altruist*, p. 16.

23. Nancy Hoffman, *Woman's "True" Profession: Voices*

from the History of Teaching (Old Westbury, NY: The Feminist Press, 1981), p. xxi.

24. Lelia Gaston Rhodes, "Profiles of the Careers of Selected Black Female Librarians," in *The Status of Women in Librarianship,* ed. Kathleen M. Heim (New York: Neal-Schuman Publishers, 1983), p. 192.

25. Margaret Gribskov, "Adelaide Pollock and the Founding of the NCAWE," in *Women Educators: Employees of Schools in Western Countries,* ed. Patricia A. Schmuck (Albany: State University of New York Press, 1987), p. 125.

26. Quoted in Katharine Phenix, "The Status of Women Librarians," *Frontiers* 9, no. 2 (1987): 36.

27. Margery W. Davies, *Women's Place Is at the Typewriter: Office Work and Office Workers, 1870–1930* (Philadelphia: Temple University Press, 1982). This analysis of the feminization of occupations at the turn of the century is consistent with the pattern described by Sam Cohn in *The Process of Occupational Sex-Typing: The Feminization of Clerical Work in Great Britain* (Philadelphia: Temple University Press, 1985). Cohn identifies three main determinants of occupational feminization in the nineteenth century: (1) organizational imperative to control labor costs; (2) lack of effective organized male employee resistance; and (3) absence of a competing labor force. All of these factors were significant in the feminization of nursing, teaching, librarianship, and social work.

28. Quoted in Madeleine R. Grumet, *Bitter Milk: Women and Teaching* (Amherst: University of Massachusetts Press, 1988), p. 39.

29. Quoted in Anita R. Schiller, "Sex and Library Careers," in *Women in Librarianship: Melvil's Rib Symposium,* ed. Margaret Myers and Mayra Scarborough (New Brunswick, NJ: Rutgers University Graduate School of Library Service, 1975), p. 16.

30. Reverby, *Ordered to Care,* p. 124.

31. Jacqueline Jones, *Labor of Love, Labor of Sorrow: Black Women, Work and the Family, from Slavery to the Present* (New York: Random House, 1985), pp. 143–45; Hine, *Black Women*

in White; Elizabeth Higginbotham, "Employment for Professional Black Women in the Twentieth Century," in *Ingredients for Women's Employment Policy,* ed. Christine Bose and Glenna Spitze (Albany: State University of New York Press, 1987), pp. 73–92.

32. Susan Ware, *Modern American Women: A Documentary History* (Chicago: Dorsey Press, 1989), p. 50.

33. Robert E. Doherty, "Tempest on the Hudson: The struggle for 'Equal Pay for Equal Work' in the New York City Public Schools, 1907–1911," *History of Education Quarterly* 19 (winter 1979), pp. 413–34; Garrison, *Apostles of Culture;* Leslie Leighninger, *Social Work: Search for Identity* (New York: Greenwood Press, 1987) p. 11.

34. Alice Kessler-Harris, *A Woman's Wage: Historical Meanings and Social Consequences* (Lexington: University of Kentucky Press, 1990). Quotes are from pp. 89 and 19.

35. Doherty, "Tempest on the Hudson."

36. Kathleen C. Berkeley, " 'The Ladies Want to Bring About Reform in the Public Schools': Public Education and Women's Rights in the Post–Civil War South," *History of Education Quarterly* 24 (spring 1984): 45–58.

37. Doherty, "Tempest on the Hudson."

38. Jean Stockard and Miriam Johnson, "The Sources and Dynamics of Sexual Inequality in the Profession of Education," in *Educational Policy and Management,* ed. Patricia Schmuck, W. W. Charters and Richard O. Carlson (New York: Academic Press, 1981), pp. 235–54; Alice Kessler-Harris, *Out to Work: A History of Wage-Earning Women in the United States* (Oxford: Oxford University Press, 1982), p. 117; Rothman, *Woman's Proper Place,* pp. 154–56.

39. Tyack and Strober, "Jobs and Gender," p. 143; Myra H. Strober and Andri Gordon Lanford, "The Feminization of Public School Teaching: Cross-Sectional Analysis, 1850–1880," *Signs* 11 (1986): 212–35.

40. Berkeley, " 'The Ladies Want to Bring About Reform.' "

41. Tyack and Strober, "Jobs and Gender," p. 143.

42. Nightingale, *Notes on Nursing,* p. 132.

43. Regina Markell Morantz-Sanchez, *Sympathy and Science: Women Physicians in American Medicine* (Oxford: Oxford University Press, 1985), p. 262.

44. Christine L. Williams, *Gender Differences at Work: Women and Men in Nontraditional Occupations* (Berkeley: University of California Press, 1989), p. 91.

45. Quoted in Schiller, "Sex and Library Careers," p. 16.

46. Salome Cutler Fairchild, "Women in American Libraries," *Library Journal* 29 (1904): 157–62; reprinted in *The Role of Women in Librarianship, 1876–1976*, pp. 53, 54.

47. Charol Shakeshaft, *Women in Educational Administration* (Newbury Park, CA: Sage, 1987), p. 40.

48. Ibid., p. 43.

49. Remarks of Miss M. E. Sargent, in "Proceedings of the Fourteenth American Library Association Conference, Lakewood," *Library Journal* 17 (August 1892): 89–94; reprinted in *The Role of Women in Librarianship, 1876–1976*, p. 16.

50. Myra Strober and David Tyack, "Why Do Women Teach and Men Manage?: A Report on Research on Schools," *Signs* 5 (1980): 500.

51. Leighninger, *Social Work*, p. 10; Mary Richmond, "The Need of a Training School in Applied Philanthropy," *Proceedings of the National Conference of Charities and Correction, 1897* (Boston: George H. Ellis, 1897); Dressel, "Patriarchy and Social Welfare Work."

52. Lois Scharf, *To Work and to Wed: Female Employment, Feminism, and the Great Depression* (Westport, CT: Greenwood Press, 1980), p. 91.

53. Nancy Cott, *The Grounding of Modern Feminism* (New Haven: Yale University Press, 1987), p. 225; Linda Blum, *Between Feminism and Labor: The Significance of the Comparable Worth Movement* (Berkeley: University of California Press, 1991), p. xx; Lillian Faderman, *Odd Girls and Twilight Lovers* (New York: Penguin, 1991), p. 327, n. 2.

54. John Ehrenreich, *The Altruistic Imagination: A History of Social Work and Social Policy in the United States* (Ithaca,

NY: Cornell University Press, 1985), pp. 203–4. Also see Carol Baines, "The Professions and an Ethic of Care," in *Women's Caring: Feminist Perspectives on Social Welfare*, ed. Carol T. Baines, Patricia M. Evans, and Sheila M. Neysmith (Toronto, Canada: McClellan and Stuart, 1991), pp. 59–60.

55. William J. Goode, "The Librarian: From Occupation to Profession?" *The Library Quarterly* 31 (1961), p. 309.

56. David Austin, "The Flexner Myth and the History of Social Work," *Social Service Review* 57 (1983): 364–65. See also Jeff Hearn, "Notes on Patriarchy: Professionalization and the Semi-Professions," *Sociology* 16 (1982): 184–202.

57. Richard L. Simpson and Ida Harper Simpson, "Women and Bureaucracy in the Semi-Professions," in *The Semi-Professions and Their Organization*, ed. Amitai Etzioni (New York: Free Press, 1969), pp. 199–200. For a somewhat different critique of this work and its influence in Great Britain, see Sandra Acker, "Women and Teaching: A Semi-Detached Sociology of a Semi-Profession," in *Gender, Class and Education*, ed. Stephen Walker and Len Barton (London: Falmer Press, 1983), pp. 123–39.

58. Talcott Parsons, *Family, Socialization and Interaction Process* (Glencoe, IL: Free Press, 1955), p. 15.

59. Harold Wilensky, "Women's Work: Economic Growth, Ideology, Structure," *Industrial Relations* 7 (May 1968): 235–48.

60. Peter Rossi, "Discussion," in *Seven Questions about the Profession of Librarianship*, ed. Philip H. Ennis and Howard W. Winger (Chicago: University of Chicago Press, 1962), p. 83.

61. Nancy Patricia O'Brien, "The Recruitment of Men into Librarianship following World War II," in *The Status of Women in Librarianship*, ed. Kathleen Heim (New York: Neal-Schuman Publishers, 1983), p. 63.

62. F. C. Ellenberg, "Elementary Teachers: Male or Female?" *Journal of Teacher Education* 26 (winter 1975): 329.

63. Patricia Cayo Sexton, *The Feminized Male* (New York: Random House, 1969), p. 121.

64. Diana Kravetz, "Sexism in a Woman's Profession," *So-*

cial Work 21 (November 1976): 422; C. Bernard Scotch, "Sex Status in Social Work: Grist for Women's Liberation," *Social Work* 16 (July 1971): 6.

65. Bonnie Garvin, "Values of Male Nursing Students," *Nursing Research* 25 (September-October 1976): 356.

66. Shirley Davis-Martin, "Research on Males in Nursing," *Journal of Nursing Education* 23 (April 1984): 164.

67. For further evidence that professional leaders explicitly argued that recruiting more men would enhance their professional status, see Baines, "The Professions and an Ethic of Care," pp. 36–72; Anita R. Schiller, "Women in Librarianship," in *Advances in Librarianship* 4 (1974): 103–47; Susan Vandiver, "A Herstory of Women in Social Work," in *Women's Issues and Social Work Practice*, ed. Elaine Norman and Arlene Mancuso (Itasca, IL: Peacock Publishers, 1980), pp. 21–38.

68. Elliot Freidson, *Professional Powers* (Chicago: University of Chicago Press, 1986).

69. Judith Lorber, *Women Physicians: Careers, Status and Power* (New York: Tavistock, 1984), p. 26.

70. Donald Auster, "Sex Differences in Attitudes toward Nursing Education," *Journal of Nursing Education* 18 (1979): 27.

71. A. S. Barter, "The Status of Women in School Administration," *The Education Digest* 25, no. 2 (1959), quoted in Sylvia-Lee Tibbetts, "Why Don't Women Aspire to Leadership Positions in Education?" in *Women in Educational Administration: A Book of Readings*, ed. Margaret C. Berry (Washington, D.C.: The National Association for Women Deans, Administrators, and Counselors, 1979), p. 2.

72. Aaron Rosenblatt et al., "Predominance of Male Authors in Social Work Publications," *Social Casework* 51 (July 1970): 421–30, quoted in Scotch, "Sex Status in Social Work," p. 8.

73. John Cary, "Overdue: Taking Issue with the Issues," *Wilson Library Bulletin* 45 (1971); reprinted in *The Role of Women in Librarianship, 1876–1976*, p. 195.

74. Barbara A. Ivy, "Identity, Power, and Hiring in a Feminized Profession," *Library Trends* 34 (1985): 292.

75. Many women workers have resisted the efforts of their leaders to "professionalize" their occupations, in part because they have interpreted these efforts as a denial of the womanly elements of their work. See, for example, Reverby, *Ordered to Care;* Cynthia Woods, "From Individual Dedication to Social Activism: Historical Development of Nursing Professionalism," in *Nursing History: The State of the Art,* ed. Christopher Maggs (London: Croom Helm, 1987), pp. 153–75; and Nancy Veeder and Joellen Hawkins, "Women in 'Women's Professions': Quiet Knowledge Builders," *Sociological Practice Review* 2 (1991): 264–74.

Chapter 3

1. Jerry Jacobs, *Revolving Doors: Sex Segregation and Women's Careers* (Stanford: Stanford University Press, 1989), pp. 78, 81; Dolores Vaz, "High School Senior Boys' Attitudes towards Nursing as a Career," *Nursing Research* 17 (1968): 533–38.

2. Jacobs, *Revolving Doors;* Margaret Mooney Marini and Mary C. Brinton, "Sex Typing in Occupational Socialization," in *Sex Segregation in the Workplace,* ed. Barbara Reskin (Washington, D.C.: National Academy Press, 1984).

3. Marini and Brinton, "Sex Typing in Occupational Socialization," p. 208.

4. Barrie Thorne, *Gender Play: Girls and Boys in School* (New Brunswick, NJ: Rutgers University Press, 1993).

5. According to a recent study of American college students, "women's career preferences have shifted away from the traditional fields of teaching, social work, homemaking and nursing, and toward business, law, medicine, science, engineering, and other careers requiring advanced degrees." Kenneth Green, "Who Wants to Be a Nurse?" *American Demographics* (January 1988): 46. This study found a 50 percent decline between 1974 and 1986 in the proportion of college women who want to be nurses.

6. Paula England, "The Failure of Human Capital Theory to Explain Occupational Sex Segregation," *Journal of Human Resources* 17 (1982): 358–70.

7. Sue Berryman and Linda Waite, "Young Women's Choice of Nontraditional Occupations," in *Ingredients for Women's Employment Policy*, ed. Christine Bose and Glenna Spitze (Albany: State University of New York Press, 1987), pp. 115–36.

8. See Sylvia Ann Hewlett, *A Lesser Life: The Myth of Women's Liberation in America* (New York: Warner Books, 1986); Ruth Sidel, *On Her Own: Growing Up in the Shadow of the American Dream* (New York: Viking, 1990); Arlie Hochschild with Anne Machung, *The Second Shift* (New York: Avon Books, 1989).

9. U.S. Department of Labor, Bureau of Labor Statistics, *Employment and Earnings* 38, no. 1 (January 1991): 18.

Chapter 4

1. Cynthia Fuchs Epstein, *Women in Law* (New York: Basic Books, 1981), p. 65.

2. An excellent account of the sexism encountered by women entering the Air Force Academy is Judith Hicks Stiehm, *Bring Me Men and Women: Mandated Change at the U.S. Air Force Academy* (Berkeley: University of California Press, 1981); for a personal account, see Capt. Carol Barkalow with Andrea Raab, *In the Men's House* (New York: Poseidon Press, 1990).

3. The classic study of tokenism is Rosabeth Moss Kanter's *Men and Women of the Corporation* (New York: Basic Books, 1977). This study has been replicated many times with different groups.

4. Lynn Zimmer, "Tokenism and Women in the Workplace," *Social Problems* 35 (1988): 64–77.

5. Not all practitioners in these occupations have these credentials, however. Many people who work in libraries and social-work agencies and who call themselves "librarians" and "social workers" have no professional training in these areas. Likewise, some teachers who work in private schools, and those who work for the government-sponsored teachers' corps, have no formal education credential. Finally, there are "nurses" who do not have their RN license: They are licensed vocational (or

practical) nurses (called LVN's or LPN's). This study includes only those who possess the formal professional credential.

6. *Library and Information Science Education Statistical Report, 1991* (Sarasota, FL: Association for Library and Information Science Education, 1991), p. 5; *Statistics on Social Work Education in the United States: 1989* (Alexandria, VA: Council on Social Work Education, 1990), p. 11; National Center for Education Statistics, *Profiles of Faculty in Higher Education Institutions, 1988* (U.S. Department of Education, August 1991), p. 136; *Nursing Data Review, 1987* (New York: National League for Nursing, 1988), p. 134.

7. Elizabeth Grauerholz, "Sexual Harassment of Women Professors by Students: Exploring the Dynamics of Power, Authority, and Gender in a University Setting," *Sex Roles* 21 (1989): 789–801.

8. For similar criticisms of tokenism theory, see Susan E. Martin, "Think Like a Man, Work Like a Dog, and Act Like a Lady: Occupational Dilemmas of Policewomen," in *The Worth of Women's Work: A Qualitative Synthesis,* ed. Anne Statham, Eleanor Miller, and Hans Mauksch (Albany: State University of New York Press, 1988), esp. pp. 206–7; Zimmer, "Tokenism and Women in the Workplace."

Chapter 5

1. Catharine MacKinnon, *Feminism Unmodified* (Cambridge: Harvard University Press, 1987), pp. 24–25.

2. Howard S. Rowland, *The Nurse's Almanac,* 2d ed. (Rockville, MD: Aspen Systems Corp., 1984), p. 153; John W. Wright, *The American Almanac of Jobs and Salaries,* 2d ed. (New York: Avon, 1984), p. 639.

3. King Research, Inc., *Library Human Resources: A Study of Supply and Demand* (Chicago: American Library Association, 1983), p. 41.

4. See, for example, Sue J. M. Freeman, *Managing Lives: Corporate Women and Social Change* (Amherst: University of Massachusetts Press, 1990).

5. Barbara Reskin and Heidi Hartmann, *Women's Work,*

Men's Work: Sex Segregation on the Job (Washington, D.C.: National Academy Press, 1986), pp. 53–56; Jerry Jacobs, *Revolving Doors: Sex Segregation and Women's Careers* (Stanford: Stanford University Press, 1989), pp. 60–63.

6. Suzanne C. Carothers and Peggy Crull, "Contrasting Sexual Harassment in Female- and Male-Dominated Occupations," in *My Troubles Are Going to Have Trouble with Me*, ed. Karen Brodkin Sacks and Dorothy Remy (New Brunswick, NJ: Rutgers University Press, 1984), pp. 219–28.

7. Patricia A. Schmuck, "Women School Employees in the United States," in *Women Educators: Employees of Schools in Western Countries* (Albany: State University of New York Press, 1987), p. 85; James W. Grimm and Robert N. Stern, "Sex Roles and Internal Labor Market Structures: The Female Semi-Professions," *Social Problems* 21 (1974): 690–705.

8. David A. Hardcastle and Arthur J. Katz, *Employment and Unemployment in Social Work: A Study of NASW Members* (Washington, D.C.: NASW, 1979), p. 41; Reginald O. York, H. Carl Henley and Dorothy N. Gamble, "Sexual Discrimination in Social Work: Is It Salary or Advancement?" *Social Work* 32 (1987): 336–40; Grimm and Stern, "Sex Roles and Internal Labor Market Structures."

9. Leigh Estabrook, "Women's Work in the Library/Information Sector," in *My Troubles Are Going to Have Trouble with Me*, ed. Karen Brodkin Sacks and Dorothy Remy (New Brunswick, NJ: Rutgers University Press, 1984), p. 165.

10. Liliane Floge and D. M. Merrill found a similar phenomenon in their study of male nurses. See "Tokenism Reconsidered: Male Nurses and Female Physicians in a Hospital Setting," *Social Forces* 64 (1986): 925–47.

11. See also Floge and Merrill, "Tokenism Reconsidered," pp. 931–32.

12. Jim Allan makes this argument in "Male Elementary Teachers: Experiences and Perspectives," in *Doing "Women's Work": Men in Nontraditional Occupations*, ed. Christine L. Williams (Newbury Park, CA: Sage Publications, 1993), pp. 113–27.

Chapter 6

1. Candace West and Don Zimmerman, "Doing Gender," *Gender & Society* 1 (1987): 125–51.

2. David H. J. Morgan, *Discovering Men* (London and New York: Routledge, 1992), p. 140.

3. For a discussion of the historical origins of the term "gender," see Joan Scott, *Gender and the Politics of History* (New York: Columbia University Press, 1988), and Robert A. Nye, *Masculinity and Male Codes of Honor in Modern France* (New York: Oxford University Press, 1993), ch. 1.

4. Examples include Diane Barrett and George Bieger, "Sex Role, Self Esteem, and Leadership Characteristics of Male and Female Teachers and Administrators," paper presented at the annual meeting of the American Education Research Association, Washington, D.C., 1987; Shirley Davis-Martin, "Research on Males in Nursing," *Journal of Nursing Education* 23 (1984): 162–64; Robert L. Turner, "Femininity and the Librarian—Another Test," *College and Research Libraries* 41 (1980): 235–41; and Pauline Wilson, *Stereotype and Status: Librarians in the United States* (Westport, CT: Greenwood Press, 1982), pp. 119–20.

5. Michael Galbraith, "Attracting Men to Nursing: What Will They Find Important in Their Career?" *Journal of Nursing Education* 30 (1991): 182–86.

6. Sandra Lipsitz Bem, *The Lenses of Gender* (New Haven: Yale University Press, 1993), p. viii.

7. This critique of trait theory is developed in Christine L. Williams, "Case studies and the sociology of gender," in *A Case for the Case Study*, ed. Joe Feagin, Anthony Orum, and Gideon Sjoberg (Chapel Hill: University of North Carolina Press, 1991), pp. 224–43.

8. Lynne Segal discusses the variants of sex role theory in *Slow Motion: Changing Masculinities, Changing Men* (New Brunswick, NJ: Rutgers University Press, 1990), pp. 65–68.

9. Cynthia Fuchs Epstein, *Deceptive Distinctions* (New Haven: Yale University Press, 1988), p. 233. Thanks to Judy Auer-

bach for pointing out this significant passage to me. For other criticisms of role theory see Segal, *Slow Motion,* pp. 66–68, and Tim Carrigan, Bob Connell, and John Lee, "Toward a New Sociology of Masculinity," *Theory and Society* 14 (September 1985): 551–603.

10. Nancy Chodorow, *The Reproduction of Mothering* (Berkeley: University of California Press, 1978).

11. Miriam Johnson, *Strong Mothers, Weak Wives* (Berkeley: University of California Press, 1988).

12. This particular insight is typically credited to Lacan and Lacanian feminists. For a good discussion of this position, see Segal, *Slow Motion,* ch. 4.

13. For in-depth discussions of the psychoanalytic theory of masculinity, see Jessica Benjamin, *The Bonds of Love: Psychoanalysis, Feminism, and the Problem of Domination* (New York: Pantheon Books, 1988); Chodorow, *Reproduction of Mothering;* Johnson, *Strong Mothers, Weak Wives.*

14. Very little research has directly assessed this claim, in part because it is still very rare in our society for men to be actively involved in childcare. Single female-headed households, which are the fastest growing alternative family form in the United States, probably reproduce the same psychological patterns found in the traditional nuclear family insofar as men are typically absent from the daily care of children. Research is also needed to assess this claim. In situations where men are forced to participate in childcare, they may exacerbate the process of gender differentiation. See Johnson, *Strong Mothers, Weak Wives,* pp. 85–86.

15. Johnson, *Strong Mothers, Weak Wives,* esp. chs. 5–6; Christine L. Williams, *Gender Differences at Work: Women and Men in Nontraditional Occupations* (Berkeley: University of California Press, 1989), p. 67.

16. Segal, *Slow Motion,* p. 103.

17. Iris Marion Young raises these objections in "Is Male Gender Identity the Cause of Male Domination?" in *Mothering:*

Essays in Feminist Theory, ed. Joyce Trebilcot (Totowa, NJ: Rowman and Allenheld, 1983), pp. 129–46.

18. R. W. Connell, *Gender and Power* (Stanford: Stanford University Press, 1987), p. 184.

19. Ibid.

20. Susan Bordo, *Unbearable Weight: Feminism, Western Culture, and the Body* (Berkeley: University of California Press, 1993), p. 239.

21. E. Anthony Rotundo, "Body and Soul: Changing Ideals of American Middle-Class Manhood, 1770–1920," *Journal of Social History* 16 (1983): 23–38.

22. Barbara Ehrenreich, *The Hearts of Men* (Garden City, NY: Anchor Books, 1984).

23. Segal, *Slow Motion,* esp. chs. 6–7.

24. Margaret Higonnet and Patrice Higonnet, "The Double Helix," in *Behind the Lines: Gender and the Two World Wars,* ed. Margaret Higonnet, Jane Jenson, Sonya Michel, and Margaret Collins Weitz (New Haven: Yale University Press, 1987), p. 34.

25. Howard S. Rowland, ed., *The Nurses' Almanac,* 2d ed. (Rockville, MD: Aspen Systems Corp., 1984), p. 153; King Research, Inc., *Library Human Resources: A Study of Supply and Demand* (Chicago: American Library Association, 1983), p. 41; Reginald O. York, H. Carl Henley, and Dorothy N. Gamble, "Sexual Discrimination in Social Work: Is it Salary or Advancement?" *Social Work* 32 (1987): 336–40; Nancy W. Veeder and Joellen W. Hawkins, "Women in 'Women's Professions': Quiet Knowledge Builders," *Sociological Practice Review* 2 (1991): 264–74.

26. Laurel Davis discusses how male cheerleaders emphasize the masculine elements of their "work" by focusing on tumbling and stunts. See "Male Cheerleaders and the Naturalization of Gender," in *Sport, Men and the Gender Order,* ed. Michael Messner and Donald Sabo (Champaign, IL: Human Kinetics Books, 1990), pp. 153–61.

27. The nurse example comes from a "natural setting": On a recent trip to the hospital, I observed this nurse identifying

214 Notes to Pages 128–38

himself as "a former Vietnam combat nurse" to all the males that were being prepped for surgery. I later had the opportunity to talk to him about this practice. He was greatly amused that I had picked up on this strategy, which he claimed was intended to put the male patients at ease about his sexuality.

28. Rosemary Pringle, "Male Secretaries," in *Doing "Women's Work": Men in Nontraditional Occupations*, ed. Christine L. Williams (Newbury Park, CA: Sage Publications, 1993), pp. 128–51.

29. For an interesting discussion of how the gendered naming of occupations is encoded in official statistics, see Margo Conk, "Accuracy, Efficiency and Bias: The Interpretation of Women's Work in the U.S. Census of Occupations, 1890–1940," *Historical Methods* 14 (1981): 65–72.

30. Johnson, *Strong Mothers, Weak Wives*, esp. ch. 5.

31. Peggy Reeves Sanday, *Fraternity Gang Rape* (New York: New York University Press, 1990), pp. 19–20.

32. This is the finding of Janet Gans, who studied a national sample of over five thousand nursing directors: She found that married female nurses were significantly less likely than unmarried female nurses to pursue higher educational credentials. Men's pursuit of these degrees was not affected by their marital status. Gans, "The Mobile Minority: Men's Success in a Woman's Profession," Ph.D. dissertation, University of Massachusetts, 1984. I discuss this study in Williams, *Gender Differences at Work*, pp. 95–98.

33. Sara E. Rix, ed., *The American Woman, 1988–1989: A Status Report* (New York: Norton, 1988), p. 343.

34. U.S. Department of Labor, Bureau of Labor Statistics, *Employment and Earnings* 38, no. 1 (January 1991): 18.

35. Catharine MacKinnon, *Toward a Feminist Theory of the State* (Cambridge: Harvard University Press, 1990), p. 224.

36. This was a common argument in the 1970s that was used by social psychologists to explain women's underrepresentation in the top positions in their occupations. This perspective claimed that talented women experienced a profound

role conflict between staying feminine and achieving occupational success. At its worst, this research "blamed the victim" for perpetuating workplace inequality. The classic statement of this perspective is Matina Horner, "Toward an Understanding of Achievement-Related Conflicts in Women," *Journal of Social Issues* 28 (1972): 157–75.

37. L. Susan Williams and Wayne J. Villemez argue that a good proportion of men who work in predominantly female occupations enter their jobs through a "trap door": They intended to pursue more traditional lines of work but for some reason ended up in "female" jobs. This probably applies less to those in the predominantly female professions compared to those in unskilled jobs since a substantial amount of planning is required to enter the professions. But some respondents who disassociate from their work did describe the "trap door" phenomenon. See Williams and Villemez, "Seekers and Finders: Male Entry and Exit in Female-Dominated Jobs," in *Doing "Women's Work": Men in Nontraditional Occupations*, ed. Christine L. Williams (Newbury Park, CA: Sage, 1993), pp. 64–90.

38. We compared our interview findings in Christine L. Williams and E. Joel Heikes, "The Importance of Researcher's Gender in the In-Depth Interview: Evidence from Two Case Studies of Male Nurses," *Gender & Society* 7 (1993): 280–91.

39. Of the seventy-six men interviewed, five told me they were gay. Not all gay men reject hegemonic masculinity. See R. W. Connell, "A Very Straight Gay: Masculinity, Homosexual Experience, and Gender," *American Sociological Review* 57 (1992): 735–51.

40. Michael Kimmel, "Men's Responses to Feminism at the Turn of the Century," *Gender & Society* 1 (1987): 261–83.

41. Susan Faludi, *Backlash: The Undeclared War against American Women* (New York: Crown, 1991), ch. 11; R. W. Connell, "Drumming Up the Wrong Tree," *Tikkun* 7 (1992): 31–36; Kay Leigh Hagan, ed., *Women Respond to the Men's Movement* (San Francisco: Pandora, 1992).

Chapter 7

1. Barbara Reskin and Heidi Hartmann, *Women's Work, Men's Work: Sex Segregation on the Job* (Washington, D.C.: National Academy Press, 1986), pp. 10–12. The 40 percent estimate is probably low because it is based on analysis of broad occupational categories that does not take into account the significant segregation *within* occupations.

2. Rosabeth Moss Kanter observed that men and women often take on characteristics associated with their jobs, suggesting a dialectical interplay between "gendered" personality traits and occupational attributes. See *Men and Women of the Corporation* (New York: Basic Books, 1977).

3. Linda Blum, *Between Feminism and Labor: The Significance of the Comparable Worth Movement* (Berkeley: University of California Press, 1991), p. 156.

4. Both the American Library Association and the National Association of Social Workers have standing committees to investigate employment discrimination against women. When I began this project, I assumed incorrectly that I would find professional committees to promote the status of men; it did not occur to me that there would be organizations to promote women's status in these predominantly female occupations. There is an association that promotes the interests of men in nursing, called the American Association for Men in Nursing, but it is not an official part of the American Nurses' Association, which is the professional licensing association for nurses in the United States.

5. These figures were calculated from U.S. Department of Commerce, Bureau of the Census, *Detailed Population Characteristics*, vol. 1, ch. D (Washington, D.C.: Government Printing Office, 1980). The proportion of blacks in social work may be exaggerated by these statistics. The occupational definition of "social worker" used by the Census Bureau includes welfare workers and pardon and parole officers, who are not considered "professional social workers" by the National Association of Social Workers. Non-degreed social workers, or "parapro-

fessionals" are more likely to be members of oppressed racial/ethnic groups. See Paula Dressel, "Patriarchy and Social Welfare Work," *Social Problems* 34 (1987): 302. A study of degreed professionals found that 89 percent of practitioners were white. See D. A. Hardcastle, *The Social Work Labor Force* (Austin: School of Social Work, University of Texas, 1987).

Racial/ethnic minorities are also overrepresented among the paraprofessional ranks of nursing, librarianship, and teaching. See Nona Glazer, "Between a Rock and a Hard Place: Women's Professional Organizations in Nursing and Class, Racial, and Ethnic Inequalities," *Gender & Society* 5 (1991): 351–72. Natalie Sokoloff assesses the changing racial composition of these professions from 1960 to 1980 in *Black Women and White Women in the Professions* (New York: Routledge, 1992).

6. The conflict between "professionalization" and racial integration in nursing is discussed in Darlene Clark Hine, *Black Women in White: Racial Conflict and Cooperation in the Nursing Profession, 1890–1950* (Bloomington: Indiana University Press, 1989).

7. Scott Swain, "Covert Intimacy: Closeness in Men's Friendships," in *Gender in Intimate Relationships*, ed. Barbara Risman and Pepper Schwartz (Belmont, CA: Wadsworth Publishing Co., 1989), pp. 71–86. My sense is that this may be a bigger issue for heterosexual men than for gay men.

8. Michael Messner criticizes the "male bonding" aspect of men's friendships in "Like Family: Power, Intimacy, and Sexuality in Male Athletes' Friendships," in *Men's Friendships*, ed. Peter Nardi (Newbury Park, CA: Sage Publications, 1992), pp. 215–37.

9. Barbara Reskin and Patricia Roos, *Job Queues, Gender Queues: Explaining Women's Inroads into Male Occupations* (Philadelphia: Temple University Press, 1990).

10. Ibid., p. 15.

11. Ibid., p. 38.

12. Alice Kessler-Harris, *A Woman's Wage: Historical Meanings and Social Consequences* (Lexington: University Press of Kentucky, 1990).

13. The 1963 Equal Pay Act requires equal salaries for men and women who perform equal work. Title VII of the 1964 Civil Rights Act also bars employment discrimination on the basis of sex as well as race, religion, and national origin. For a discussion of these laws, see Deborah Rhode, *Justice and Gender* (Cambridge: Harvard University Press, 1989), esp. pt. 2.

14. The efforts of these occupations to "professionalize" are viewed by some as efforts to "masculinize" the jobs. See, for example, Janet Chafetz, "Women in Social Work," *Social Work* 17 (1972): 12–15. Professionalization resulted in conflicts in the nursing profession between what Susan Reverby calls "traditionalists" (those who value the "womanly" components of their jobs) and "rationalizers" (who emphasize the technical and instrumental aspects). See Reverby, *Ordered to Care: The Dilemma of American Nursing, 1850–1945* (Cambridge: Cambridge University Press, 1987). Home economists struggled with the same issues. See Teresa Strathman and Christine Williams, "Professionalizing Private Tasks: Status Building Strategies in Nursing and Home Economics," paper presented at the annual meeting of the American Sociological Association, Atlanta, Georgia, August 1988.

15. Women also suffer a wage penalty for working in predominantly female jobs, but it is less extreme than the penalty suffered by men. Within every occupation, however, men do earn more than women. These wage effects are reviewed in Paula England and Melissa Herbert, "The Pay of Men in Female Occupations: Is Comparable Worth Only for Women?" in *Doing "Women's Work": Men in Nontraditional Occupations,* ed. Christine L. Williams (Newbury Park, CA: Sage Publications, 1993), pp. 28–48.

16. The limited evidence available indicates that men who leave predominantly female occupations do increase their salaries; some of these men probably leave because they are offered higher incomes in other fields. See L. Susan Williams and Wayne J. Villemez, "Seekers and Finders: Male Entry and Exit in Female-Dominated Jobs," in *Doing "Women's Work": Men in*

Nontraditional Occupations, ed. Christine L. Williams (Newbury Park, CA: Sage Publications, 1993), pp. 64–90.

17. I hesitate to generalize about the proportions of gay men in these occupations. Certainly the stereotype is that gays are overrepresented in these occupations, but my impression is that the percentage of gays and lesbians in these fields is no higher than in other occupations. Five of the seventy-six men interviewed told me they were gay. Two of the twenty-three women in the sample told me they were lesbians. I did not directly ask respondents about their sexual orientation, although I did ask about their marital status. About 80 percent of the men in the sample were married; about 87 percent of the women were.

18. Harriet Bradley, "Across the Great Divide: The Entry of Men into 'Women's Jobs,'" in *Doing "Women's Work": Men in Nontraditional Occupations,* ed. Christine L. Williams (Newbury Park, CA: Sage Publications, 1993), pp. 10–27.

19. Jerry A. Jacobs, "Men in Female-Dominated Fields: Trends and Turnover," in *Doing "Women's Work": Men in Nontraditional Occupations,* ed. Christine L. Williams (Newbury Park, CA: Sage Publications, 1993), p. 51; Blum, *Between Feminism and Labor,* p. 154.

20. Cynthia Fuchs Epstein, "Workplace Boundaries: Conceptions and Creations," *Social Research* 56 (1989): 571–90.

21. Janice Yoder discusses how women in nontraditional occupations often attempt to minimize their difference from men in "Women at West Point: Lessons for Token Women in Male-Dominated Occupations," in *Women: A Feminist Perspective,* ed. Jo Freeman (Mountain View, CA: Mayfield Publishing Co., 1989), pp. 523–37.

Chapter 8

1. For a critique of organizational theory along these lines, see Joan Acker, "Hierarchies, Jobs, Bodies: A Theory of Gendered Organizations" *Gender & Society* 4 (June 1990): 139–58; Cynthia Cockburn, "Men's Power in Organizations: 'Equal Op-

portunities' Intervenes," in *Men, Masculinities, and Social Theory*, ed. Jeff Hearn and David Morgan (London: Unwin Hyman, 1990), pp. 72–89; David Morgan, *Discovering Men* (London: Routledge, 1992), ch. 4.

2. Joan Acker, "Hierarchies, Jobs, Bodies," p. 145.

3. Georg Simmel, *On Individuality and Social Forms* (Chicago: University of Chicago Press, 1970).

4. Rosabeth Moss Kanter, *Men and Women of the Corporation* (New York: Basic Books, 1977).

5. Jessica Benjamin, *The Bonds of Love: Psychoanalysis, Feminism, and the Problem of Domination* (New York: Pantheon Books, 1988); Nancy Chodorow, *Reproduction of Mothering* (Berkeley: University of California Press, 1978); Miriam Johnson, *Strong Mothers, Weak Wives* (Berkeley: University of California Press, 1988).

6. Christine L. Williams, *Gender Differences at Work: Women and Men in Nontraditional Occupations* (Berkeley: University of California Press, 1989).

7. Christine L. Williams, "Psychoanalytic Theory and the Sociology of Gender," in *Theory on Gender/Feminism on Theory*, ed. Paula England (New York: Aldine de Gruyter, 1993), pp. 131–49.

8. Lynne Segal, *Slow Motion: Changing Masculinities, Changing Men* (New Brunswick, NJ: Rutgers University Press, 1990).

Appendix

1. This is described in Anselm Strauss, *Qualitative Analysis for Social Scientists* (Cambridge: Cambridge University Press, 1987).

2. Christine L. Williams and E. Joel Heikes, "The Importance of Researcher's Gender in the In-Depth Interview: Evidence from Two Case Studies of Male Nurses," *Gender & Society* 7 (1993): 280–91.

3. I discuss these objections in "Psychoanalytic Theory and the Sociology of Gender," in *Theory on Gender/Feminism on Theory*, ed. Paula England (New York: Aldine de Gruyter, 1993), pp. 140–42.

Bibliography

Abbott, Pamela, and Claire Wallace, eds. *The Sociology of the Caring Professions*. London: Falmer Press, 1990.

Acker, Joan. "Hierarchies, Jobs, Bodies: A Theory of Gendered Organizations." *Gender & Society* 4 (June 1990): 139–58.

Acker, Sandra. "Women and Teaching: A Semi-Detached Sociology of a Semi-Profession." Pp. 123–39 in *Gender, Class and Education*, ed. Stephen Walker and Len Barton. London: Falmer Press, 1983.

Allan, Jim. "Male Elementary Teachers: Experiences and Perspectives." Pp. 113–27 in *Doing "Women's Work": Men in Nontraditional Occupations*, ed. Christine L. Williams. Newbury Park, CA: Sage Publications, 1993.

Angoff, Allan. "The Male Librarian—An Anomaly?" *Library Journal* (February 15, 1959): 553–56.

Auster, Donald. "Sex Differences in Attitudes toward Nursing Education." *Journal of Nursing Education* 18 (1979): 19–28.

Austin, David. "The Flexner Myth and the History of Social Work." *Social Service Review* 57 (1983): 357–77.

Baines, Carol. "The Professions and an Ethic of Care." Pp. 36–72 in *Women's Caring: Feminist Perspectives on Social Welfare*, ed. Carol T. Baines, Patricia M. Evans, and Sheila M. Neysmith. Toronto, Canada: McClellan and Stuart, 1991.

Barkalow, Carol, with Andrea Raab. *In the Men's House*. New York: Poseidon Press, 1990.

Baron, Ava. "Gender and Labor History: Learning from the Past, Looking to the Future." Pp. 1–46 in *Work Engendered:*

Toward a New History of American Labor, ed. Ava Baron. Ithaca, NY: Cornell University Press, 1991.

Barrett, Diane, and George Bieger. "Sex Role, Self Esteem, and Leadership Characteristics of Male and Female Teachers and Administrators." Paper presented at the annual meeting of the American Education Research Association, Washington, D.C., 1987.

Beatty, Barbara. " 'A Vocation from on High': Kindergartning as an Occupation for American Women." Pp. 35–50 in *Changing Education: Women as Radicals and Conservators,* ed. Joyce Antler and Sari Knopp Biklin. Albany: State University of New York Press, 1990.

Bem, Sandra Lipsitz. *The Lenses of Gender.* New Haven: Yale University Press, 1993.

Benjamin, Jessica. *The Bonds of Love: Psychoanalysis, Feminism, and the Problem of Domination.* New York: Pantheon Books, 1988.

Berkeley, Kathleen C. " 'The Ladies Want to Bring About Reform in the Public Schools': Public Education and Women's Rights in the Post–Civil War South." *History of Education Quarterly* 24 (spring 1984): 45–58.

Berryman, Sue, and Linda Waite. "Young Women's Choice of Nontraditional Occupations." Pp. 115–36 in *Ingredients for Women's Employment Policy,* ed. Christine Bose and Glenna Spitze. Albany: State University of New York Press, 1987.

Bielby, William T., and James N. Baron. "A Woman's Place Is with Other Women: Sex Segregation within Organizations." Pp. 27–55 in *Sex Segregation in the Workplace: Trends, Explanations, Remedies,* ed. Barbara Reskin. Washington, D.C.: National Academy Press, 1984.

Blau, Francine D., and Anne E. Winkler. "Women in the Labor Force: An Overview." Pp. 265–86 in *Women: A Feminist Perspective,* ed. Jo Freeman. 4th ed. Mountain View, CA: Mayfield Publishing Co., 1989.

Blum, Linda. *Between Feminism and Labor: The Significance of the Comparable Worth Movement.* Berkeley: University of California Press, 1991.

Blumer, Herbert. *Symbolic Interactionism: Perspective and Method.* Berkeley: University of California Press, 1969.

Bordo, Susan. *Unbearable Weight: Feminism, Western Culture, and the Body.* Berkeley: University of California Press, 1993.

Bradley, Harriet. "Across the Great Divide: The Entry of Men into Women's Jobs." Pp. 10–27 in *Doing "Women's Work": Men in Nontraditional Occupations,* ed. Christine L. Williams. Newbury Park, CA: Sage, 1993.

Brumberg, Joan J., and Nancy Tomes. "Women in the Professions: A Research Agenda for American Historians." *Reviews in American History* 10 (June 1982): 275–96.

Carothers, Suzanne C., and Peggy Crull. "Contrasting Sexual Harassment in Female- and Male-Dominated Occupations." Pp. 219–28 in *My Troubles Are Going to Have Trouble with Me,* ed. Karen Brodkin Sacks and Dorothy Remy. New Brunswick, NJ: Rutgers University Press, 1984.

Carrigan, Tim, Bob Connell, and John Lee. "Toward a New Sociology of Masculinity." *Theory and Society* 14 (1985): 551–603.

Chafetz, Janet. "Women in Social Work." *Social Work* 17 (1972): 12–15.

Charles, Maria. "Cross-National Variation in Occupational Sex Segregation." *American Sociological Review* 57 (1992): 483–502.

Chodorow, Nancy. *The Reproduction of Mothering.* Berkeley: University of California Press, 1978.

Cockburn, Cynthia. "The Gendering of Jobs: Workplace Relations and the Reproduction of Sex Segregation." Pp. 29–42 in *Gender Segregation at Work,* ed. Sylvia Walby. Philadelphia: Open University Press, 1988.

———. *In the Way of Women.* New York: ILR Press, 1991.

———. "Men's Power in Organizations: 'Equal Opportunities' Intervenes." Pp. 72–89 in *Men, Masculinities, and Social Theory,* ed. Jeff Hearn and David Morgan. London: Unwin Hyman, 1990.

Cohen, Deborah L. "Looking for a Few Good Men: Why Are There So Few Male Teachers in the Early Grades?" *Teacher Magazine* 2 (1990): 14–15.

Cohn, Sam. *The Process of Occupational Sex-Typing: The Feminization of Clerical Work in Great Britain.* Philadelphia: Temple University Press, 1985.

Conk, Margo. "Accuracy, Efficiency and Bias: The Interpretation of Women's Work in the U.S. Census of Occupations, 1890–1940." *Historical Methods* 14 (1981): 65–72.

Connell, R. W. "Drumming Up the Wrong Tree." *Tikkun* 7 (1992): 31–36.

———. *Gender and Power*. Stanford: Stanford University Press, 1987.

———. "A Very Straight Gay: Masculinity, Homosexual Experience, and Gender." *American Sociological Review* 57 (1992): 735–51.

Cott, Nancy. *The Grounding of Modern Feminism*. New Haven: Yale University Press, 1987.

Cowan, Ruth Schwartz. *More Work for Mother*. New York: Basic, 1983.

Davies, Margery W. *Women's Place Is at the Typewriter: Office Work and Office Workers, 1870–1930*. Philadelphia: Temple University Press, 1982.

Davis, Laurel R. "Male Cheerleaders and the Naturalization of Gender." Pp. 153–61 in *Sport, Men and the Gender Order*, ed. Michael Messner and Donald Sabo. Champaign, IL: Human Kinetics Books, 1990.

Davis-Martin, Shirley. "Research on Males in Nursing." *Journal of Nursing Education* 23 (April 1984): 162–64.

Deaux, Kay, and Joseph Ullman. *Women of Steel*. New York: Praeger, 1983.

Doherty, Robert E. "Tempest on the Hudson: The Struggle for 'Equal Pay for Equal Work' in the New York City Public Schools, 1907–1911." *History of Education Quarterly* 19, no. 4 (1979): 413–34.

Dressel, Paula. "Patriarchy and Social Welfare Work." *Social Problems* 34 (June 1987): 294–309.

Ehrenreich, Barbara. *The Hearts of Men*. Garden City, NY: Anchor Books, 1984.

Ehrenreich, John. *The Altruistic Imagination: A History of Social Work and Social Policy in the United States*. Ithaca, NY: Cornell University Press, 1985.

Ellenberg, F. C. "Elementary Teachers: Male or Female?" *Journal of Teacher Education* 26, no. 4 (1975): 329–34.

England, Paula. *Comparable Worth: Theories and Evidence.* Hawthorne, NY: Aldine de Gruyter, 1992.

——. "The Failure of Human Capital Theory to Explain Occupational Sex Segregation." *Journal of Human Resources* 17 (1982): 358–70.

England, Paula, and Melissa Herbert. "The Pay of Men in Female Occupations: Is Comparable Worth Only for Women?" Pp. 28–48 in *Doing "Women's Work": Men in Nontraditional Occupations*, ed. Christine L. Williams. Newbury Park, CA: Sage, 1993.

Epstein, Cynthia Fuchs. *Deceptive Distinctions.* New Haven: Yale University Press, 1988.

——. *Women in Law.* New York: Basic Books, 1981.

——. "Workplace Boundaries: Conceptions and Creations." *Social Research* 56 (1989): 571–90.

Estabrook, Leigh. "Women's Work in the Library/Information Sector." Pp. 160–72 in *My Troubles Are Going to Have Trouble with Me*, ed. Karen Brodkin Sacks and Dorothy Remy. New Brunswick, NJ: Rutgers University Press, 1984.

Faderman, Lillian. *Odd Girls and Twilight Lovers: A History of Lesbian Life in Twentieth-Century America.* New York: Penguin, 1991.

Faludi, Susan. *Backlash: The Undeclared War against American Women.* New York: Crown, 1991.

Floge, Liliane, and D. M. Merrill. "Tokenism Reconsidered: Male Nurses and Female Physicians in a Hospital Setting." *Social Forces* 64 (1986): 925–47.

Freeman, Sue J. M. *Managing Lives: Corporate Women and Social Change.* Amherst: University of Massachusetts Press, 1990.

Freidson, Elliot. *Professional Powers.* Chicago: University of Chicago Press, 1986.

Galbraith, Michael. "Attracting Men to Nursing: What Will They Find Important in Their Career?" *Journal of Nursing Education* 30 (1991): 182–86.

Gans, Janet. "The Mobile Minority: Men's Success in a Woman's Profession." Ph.D. dissertation, University of Massachusetts, 1984.

Garrison, Dee. *Apostles of Culture: The Public Librarian and American Society, 1876–1920.* New York: The Free Press, 1979.

———. "The Tender Technicians: The Feminization of Public Librarianship, 1876–1905." *Journal of Social History* 6 (1972–73): 133–59.

Garvin, Bonnie. "Values of Male Nursing Students." *Nursing Research* 25 (September-October 1976): 352–57.

Glazer, Nona Y. "Between a Rock and a Hard Place: Women's Professional Organizations in Nursing and Class, Racial, and Ethnic Inequalities." *Gender & Society* 5 (1991): 351–72.

Glazer, Penina Migdal, and Miriam Slater. *Unequal Colleagues: The Entrance of Women into the Professions, 1890–1940.* New Brunswick, NJ: Rutgers University Press, 1987.

Goode, William. "The Librarian: From Occupation to Profession?" *The Library Quarterly* 31 (1961): 306–18.

Grauerholz, Elizabeth. "Sexual Harassment of Women Professors by Students: Explaining the Dynamics of Power, Authority, and Gender in a University Setting." *Sex Roles* 21 (1989): 789–801.

Green, Kenneth. "Who Wants to Be a Nurse?" *American Demographics* (January 1988): 46–48, 61.

Gribskov, Margaret. "Adelaide Pollock and the Founding of the NCAWE." Pp. 121–37 in *Women Educators: Employees of Schools in Western Countries,* ed. Patricia A. Schmuck. Albany: State University of New York Press, 1987.

Grimm, James W., and Robert N. Stern. "Sex Roles and Internal Labor Market Structures: The Female Semi-Professions." *Social Problems* 21 (1974): 690–705.

Grumet, Madeleine R. *Bitter Milk: Women and Teaching.* Amherst: University of Massachusetts Press, 1988.

Gutek, Barbara. *Sex and the Workplace.* San Francisco: Jossey-Bass, 1985.

Hagan, Kay Leigh, ed. *Women Respond to the Men's Movement.* San Francisco: Pandora, 1992.

Hall, Elaine J. "Smiling, Deferring, and Flirting: Doing Gender by Giving 'Good Service.' " *Work and Occupations* 20 (1993): 452–71.

Hardcastle, David A. *The Social Work Labor Force.* Austin: School of Social Work, University of Texas, 1987.

Hardcastle, David A., and Arthur J. Katz. *Employment and Unemployment in Social Work: A Study of NASW Members.* Washington, D.C.: National Association of Social Workers, 1979.

Hartmann, Heidi. "Capitalism, Patriarchy, and Job Segregation by Sex." Pp. 206–47 in *Capitalist Patriarchy and the Case for Socialist Feminism,* ed. Zillah Eisenstein. New York: Monthly Review Press, 1979.

Hearn, Jeff. "Notes on Patriarchy: Professionalization and the Semi-Professions." *Sociology* 16 (1982): 184–202.

Hearn, Jeff, and Wendy Parkin. *Sex at Work: The Power and Paradox of Organization Sexuality.* New York: St. Martin's, 1987.

Hewlett, Sylvia Ann. *A Lesser Life: The Myth of Women's Liberation in America.* New York: Warner Books, 1986.

Higginbotham, Elizabeth. "Employment for Professional Black Women in the Twentieth Century." Pp. 73–92 in *Ingredients for Women's Employment Policy,* ed. Christine Bose and Glenna Spitze. Albany: State University of New York Press, 1987.

Higonnet, Margaret, and Patrice Higonnet. "The Double Helix." Pp. 31–47 in *Behind the Lines: Gender and the Two World Wars,* ed. Margaret Higonnet, Jane Jenson, Sonya Michel, and Margaret Collins Weitz. New Haven: Yale University Press, 1987.

Hine, Darlene Clark. *Black Women in White: Racial Conflict and Cooperation in the Nursing Profession, 1890–1950.* Bloomington: Indiana University Press, 1989.

Hochschild, Arlie, with Anne Machung. *The Second Shift.* New York: Avon Books, 1989.

Hoffman, Nancy. *Women's "True" Profession: Voices from the History of Teaching.* Old Westbury, NY: The Feminist Press, 1981.

Hoffmann, Frances L. "Feminism and Nursing." *NWSA Journal* 3 (1991): 53–69.

Horner, Matina. "Toward an Understanding of Achievement-

Related Conflicts in Women." *Journal of Social Issues* 28 (1972): 157–75.

Ivy, Barbara A. "Identity, Power, and Hiring in a Feminized Profession." *Library Trends* 34 (1985): 291–308.

Jacobs, Jerry A. "Men in Female-Dominated Fields: Trends and Turnover." Pp. 49–63 in *Doing "Women's Work": Men in Nontraditional Occupations,* ed. Christine L. Williams. Newbury Park, CA: Sage, 1993.

———. *Revolving Doors: Sex Segregation and Women's Careers.* Stanford: Stanford University Press, 1989.

Johnson, Miriam. *Strong Mothers, Weak Wives.* Berkeley: University of California Press, 1988.

Jones, Jacqueline. *Labor of Love, Labor of Sorrow: Black Women, Work and the Family, from Slavery to the Present.* New York: Random House, 1985.

Kanter, Rosabeth Moss. *Men and Women of the Corporation.* New York: Basic Books, 1977.

Kerber, Linda K. *Women of the Republic: Intellect and Ideology in Revolutionary America.* New York: Norton, 1986.

Kessler-Harris, Alice. *Out to Work: A History of Wage-Earning Women in the United States.* Oxford: Oxford University Press, 1982.

———. *A Woman's Wage: Historical Meanings and Social Consequences.* Lexington: University of Kentucky Press, 1990.

Kimmel, Michael. "Men's Responses to Feminism at the Turn of the Century." *Gender & Society* 1 (1987): 261–83.

King Research, Inc. *Library Human Resources: A Study of Supply and Demand.* Chicago: American Library Association, 1983.

Kravetz, Diana. "Sexism in a Woman's Profession." *Social Work* 21 (November 1976): 421–26.

Leidner, Robin. *Fast Food, Fast Talk.* Berkeley: University of California Press, 1993.

Leighninger, Leslie. *Social Work: Search for Identity.* New York: Greenwood Press, 1987.

Library and Information Science Education Statistical Report, 1991. Sarasota, FL: Association for Library and Information Science Education, 1991.

Lorber, Judith. *Women Physicians: Careers, Status and Power.* New York: Tavistock, 1984.

Lubove, Roy. *The Professional Altruist: The Emergence of Social Work as a Career, 1880–1930.* New York: Atheneum, 1975.

MacKinnon, Catharine. *Feminism Unmodified.* Cambridge: Harvard University Press, 1987.

———. *Toward a Feminist Theory of the State.* Cambridge: Harvard University Press, 1990.

Mann, Horace. *Eighth Annual Report of the Board of Education.* P. 268 in *Women in the American Economy,* ed. W. Elliot Brownlee and Mary M. Brownlee. New Haven: Yale University Press, 1976.

Margolis, Maxine. *Mothers and Such.* Berkeley: University of California Press, 1984.

Marini, Margaret Mooney. "Sex Differences in Earnings in the United States." *Annual Review of Sociology* 15 (1989): 343–80.

Marini, Margaret Mooney, and Mary C. Brinton. "Sex Typing in Occupational Socialization." Pp. 192–232 in *Sex Segregation in the Workplace,* ed. Barbara Reskin. Washington, D.C.: National Academy Press, 1984.

Martin, Susan E. *Breaking and Entering: Policewomen on Patrol.* Berkeley: University of California Press, 1980.

———. "Think Like a Man, Work Like a Dog, and Act Like a Lady: Occupational Dilemmas of Policewomen." Pp. 205–23 in *The Worth of Women's Work: A Qualitative Synthesis,* ed. Anne Statham, Eleanor Miller, and Hans Mauksch. Albany: State University of New York Press, 1988.

Messner, Michael. "Like Family: Power, Intimacy, and Sexuality in Male Athletes' Friendships." Pp. 215–37 in *Men's Friendships,* ed. Peter Nardi. Newbury Park, CA: Sage, 1992.

Morantz-Sanchez, Regina Markell. *Sympathy and Science: Women Physicians in American Medicine.* Oxford: Oxford University Press, 1985.

Morgan, David H. J. *Discovering Men.* London and New York: Routledge, 1992.

National Center for Education Statistics. *Profiles of Faculty in Higher Education Institutions, 1988.* Washington, D.C.: U.S. Dept. of Education, 1990.

Nightingale, Florence. *Notes on Nursing*. 1860. Reprint, New York: Dover, 1969.

Nursing Data Review, 1987. New York: National League for Nursing, 1988.

Nye, Robert A. *Masculinity and Male Codes of Honor in Modern France*. New York: Oxford University Press, 1993.

O'Brien, Nancy Patricia. "The Recruitment of Men into Librarianship following World War II." Pp. 51–66 in *The Status of Women in Librarianship*, ed. Kathleen Heim. New York: Neal-Schuman Publishers, 1983.

Parsons, Talcott. *Family, Socialization and Interaction Process*. Glencoe, IL: Free Press, 1955.

Phenix, Katharine. "The Status of Women Librarians." *Frontiers* 9 (1987): 36–40.

Pringle, Rosemary. "Male Secretaries." Pp. 152–67 in *Doing "Women's Work": Men in Nontraditional Occupations*, ed. Christine L. Williams. Newbury Park, CA: Sage Publications, 1993.

———. *Secretaries Talk*. New York: Verso, 1988.

Raunch, Julia. "Women in Social Work: Friendly Visitors in Philadelphia, 1880." *Social Service Review* 49 (1975): 241–59.

Reskin, Barbara. "Bringing the Men Back In: Sex Differentiation and the Devaluation of Women's Work." *Gender & Society* 2 (1988): 58–81.

———, ed. *Sex Segregation in the Workplace: Trends, Explanations, Remedies*. Washington, D.C.: National Academy Press, 1984.

Reskin, Barbara, and Heidi Hartmann. *Women's Work, Men's Work: Sex Segregation on the Job*. Washington, D.C.: National Academy Press, 1986.

Reskin, Barbara, and Polly Phipps. "Women in Male-Dominated Professional and Managerial Occupations." Pp. 190–205 in *Women Working*, ed. Ann Helton Stromberg and Shirley Harkess. Mountain View, CA: Mayfield Publishing Co., 1988.

Reskin, Barbara, and Patricia Roos. *Job Queues, Gender Queues*. Philadelphia: Temple University Press, 1990.

Reverby, Susan. *Ordered to Care: The Dilemma of American Nursing, 1850–1945*. Cambridge: Cambridge University Press, 1987.

Rhode, Deborah. *Justice and Gender*. Cambridge: Harvard University Press, 1989.

Rhodes, Lelia Gaston. "Profiles of the Careers of Selected Black Female Librarians." Pp. 191–206 in *The Status of Women in Librarianship*, ed. Kathleen M. Heim. New York: Neal-Schuman Publishers, 1983.

Richmond, Mary. "The Need of a Training School in Applied Philanthropy." *Proceedings of the National Conference of Charities and Correction, 1897*. Boston: George H. Ellis, 1897.

Rix, Sara E., ed. *The American Woman, 1988–89: A Status Report*. New York: Norton, 1988.

Rogers, Margaret L. "Private Nursing." *American Journal of Nursing* 2 (1901): 82–85.

The Role of Women in Librarianship, 1876–1976 (reprinted essays and addresses), ed. Kathleen Weibel and Kathleen M. Heim. Phoenix, AZ: Oryx Press, 1979.

Rossi, Peter. "Discussion." Pp. 82–83 in *Seven Questions about the Profession of Librarianship*, ed. Philip H. Ennis and Howard W. Winger. Chicago: University of Chicago Press, 1962.

Rothman, Sheila. *Women's Proper Place*. New York: Basic Books, 1978.

Rotundo, E. Antonio. *American Manhood: Transformations in Masculinity from the Revolution to the Modern Era*. New York: Basic Books, 1993.

———. "Body and Soul: Changing Ideals of American Middle-Class Manhood, 1770–1920." *Journal of Social History* 16 (1983): 23–38.

Rowland, Howard S. *The Nurses' Almanac*. 2d ed. Rockville, MD: Aspen Systems Corp., 1984.

Ryan, Mary P. *Womanhood in America*. 2d ed. New York: New Viewpoints, 1978.

Sanday, Peggy Reeves. *Fraternity Gang Rape*. New York: New York University Press, 1990.

Scharf, Lois. *To Work and to Wed: Female Employment, Femi-

nism, and the Great Depression. Westport, CT: Greenwood Press, 1980.

Schiller, Anita R. "Sex and Library Careers." Pp. 11–22 in *Women in Librarianship: Melvil's Rib Symposium*, ed. Margaret Myers and Mayra Scarborough. New Brunswick, NJ: Rutgers University Graduate School of Library Service, 1975.

———. "Women in Librarianship." *Advances in Librarianship* 4 (1974): 103–47.

Schmuck, Patricia A. "Women School Employees in the United States." Pp. 75–97 in *Women Educators: Employees of Schools in Western Countries*. Albany: State University of New York Press, 1987.

Schreiber, Carol Tropp. *Changing Places: Men and Women in Transitional Occupations*. Cambridge: MIT Press, 1979.

Scotch, C. Bernard. "Sex Status in Social Work: Grist for Women's Liberation." *Social Work* 16 (July 1971): 5–11.

Scott, Joan. *Gender and the Politics of History*. New York: Columbia University Press, 1988.

———. "Gender: A Useful Category for Historical Analysis." *American Historical Review* 91 (1986): 1053–75.

Segal, Lynne. *Slow Motion: Changing Masculinities, Changing Men*. New Brunswick, NJ: Rutgers University Press, 1990.

Sexton, Patricia Cayo. *The Feminized Male*. New York: Random House, 1969.

Shakeshaft, Charol. *Women in Educational Administration*. Newbury Park, CA: Sage, 1987.

Sidel, Ruth. *On Her Own: Growing Up in the Shadow of the American Dream*. New York: Viking, 1990.

Simmel, Georg. *On Individuality and Social Forms*. Chicago: University of Chicago Press, 1970.

Simpson, Richard L., and Ida Harper Simpson. "Women and Bureaucracy in the Semi-Professions." Pp. 196–265 in *The Semi-Professions and Their Organization*, ed. Amitai Etzioni. New York: Free Press, 1969.

Sklar, Kathryn Kish, *Catharine Beecher: A Study in American Domesticity*. New Haven: Yale University Press, 1973.

Sokoloff, Natalie. *Between Money and Love*. New York: Praeger, 1980.

————. *Black Women and White Women in the Professions*. New York: Routledge, 1992.

Statistics on Social Work Education in the United States: 1989. Alexandria, VA: Council on Social Work Education, 1990.

Stiehm, Judith Hicks. *Arms and the Enlisted Woman*. Philadelphia: Temple University Press, 1989.

————. *Bring Me Men and Women: Mandated Change at the U.S. Air Force Academy*. Berkeley: University of California Press, 1981.

Stockard, Jean, and Miriam Johnson. "The Sources and Dynamics of Sexual Inequality in the Profession of Education." Pp. 235–54 in *Educational Policy and Management*, ed. Patricia Schmuck, W. W. Charters and Richard O. Carlson. New York: Academic Press, 1981.

Strathman, Teresa, and Christine L. Williams. "Professionalizing Private Tasks: Status Building Strategies in Nursing and Home Economics." Paper presented at the annual meeting of the American Sociological Association, Atlanta, Georgia, 1988.

Strauss, Anselm. *Qualitative Analysis for Social Scientists*. Cambridge: Cambridge University Press, 1987.

Strober, Myra H., and Andri Gordon Landord. "The Feminization of Public School Teaching: Cross-Sectional Analysis, 1850–1880." *Signs* 11 (1986): 212–35.

Strober, Myra H., and David Tyack. "Why Do Women Teach and Men Manage?: A Report on Research on Schools." *Signs* 5 (1980): 494–503.

Sugg, Redding S. *Motherteacher: The Feminization of American Education*. Charlottesville: University Press of Virginia, 1978.

Swain, Scott. "Covert Intimacy: Closeness in Men's Friendships." Pp. 71–86 in *Gender in Intimate Relationships*, ed. Barbara Risman and Pepper Schwartz. Belmont, CA: Wadsworth Publishing Co., 1989.

Thorne, Barrie, *Gender Play: Girls and Boys in School*. New Brunswick, NJ: Rutgers University Press, 1993.

Tibbetts, Sylvia-Lee. "Why Don't Women Aspire to Leadership Positions in Education?" Pp. 1–11 in *Women in Educational*

Administration: A Book of Readings, ed. Margaret C. Berry. Washington, D.C.: National Association for Women Deans, Administrators, and Counselors, 1979.

Turner, Robert L. "Femininity and the Librarian—Another Test." *College and Research Libraries* 41 (1980): 235–41.

Tyack, David, and Myra Strober. "Jobs and Gender: A History of the Structuring of Educational Employment by Sex." Pp. 131–52 of *Educational Policy and Management,* ed. Patricia Schmuck, W. W. Charters and Richard O. Carlson. New York: Academic Press, 1981.

U.S. Department of Commerce. Bureau of the Census. *Detailed Population Characteristics.* Vol. 1, ch. D. Washington, D.C.: Government Printing Office, 1980.

U.S. Department of Labor. Bureau of Labor Statistics. *Employment and Earnings.* Vols. 38, 40.

Vandiver, Susan. "A Herstory of Women in Social Work." Pp. 21–38 in *Women's Issues and Social Work Practice,* ed. Elaine Norman and Arlene Mancuso. Itasca, IL: Peacock Publishers, 1980.

Vaz, Dolores. "High School Senior Boys' Attitudes Towards Nursing as a Career." *Nursing Research* 17 (1968): 533–38.

Veeder, Nancy W. and Joellen W. Hawkins. "Women in 'Women's Professions': Quiet Knowledge Builders." *Sociological Practice Review* 2 (1991): 264–74.

Vicinus, Martha. *Independent Women: Work and Community for Single Women, 1850–1920.* Chicago: University of Chicago Press, 1985.

Ware, Susan. *Modern American Women: A Documentary History.* Chicago: Dorsey Press, 1989.

Weibel, Kathleen. "Towards a Feminist Profession." *Library Journal* 101 (1976): 263–67.

West, Candace, and Don Zimmerman. "Doing Gender." *Gender & Society* 1 (1987): 125–51.

Wharton, Amy S., and James N. Baron. "So Happy Together? The Impact of Gender Segregation on Men at Work." *American Sociological Review* 52 (1987): 574–87.

Wilensky, Harold. "Women's Work: Economic Growth, Ideology, Structure." *Industrial Relations* 7 (May 1968): 235–48.

Williams, Christine L. "Case Studies and the Sociology of Gender." Pp. 224–43 in *A Case for the Case Study*, ed. Joe Feagin, Anthony Orum, and Gideon Sjoberg. Chapel Hill: University of North Carolina Press, 1991.

———. *Gender Differences at Work: Women and Men in Nontraditional Occupations*. Berkeley: University of California Press, 1989.

———. "The Glass Escalator: Hidden Advantages for Men in the Female Professions." *Social Problems* 39 (1992): 253–67.

———. "Psychoanalytic Theory and the Sociology of Gender." Pp. 131–49 in *Theory on Gender/Feminism on Theory*, ed. Paula England. New York: Aldine de Gruyter, 1993.

———, ed. *Doing "Women's Work": Men in Nontraditional Occupations* (Newbury Park, CA: Sage Publications, 1993).

Williams, Christine L., and E. Joel Heikes. "The Importance of Researcher's Gender in the In-Depth Interview: Evidence from Two Case Studies of Male Nurses." *Gender & Society* 7 (1993): 280–91.

Williams, L. Susan, and Wayne J. Villemez. "Seekers and Finders: Male Entry and Exit in Female-Dominated Jobs." Pp. 64–90 in *Doing "Women's Work": Men in Nontraditional Occupations*, ed. Christine L. Williams. Newbury Park, CA: Sage Publications, 1993.

Wilson, Pauline. *Stereotype and Status: Librarians in the United States*. Westport, CT: Greenwood Press, 1982.

Woods, Cynthia Q. "From Individual Dedication to Social Activism: Historical Development of Nursing Professionalism." Pp. 153–75 of *Nursing History: The State of the Art*, ed. Christopher Maggs. London: Croom Helm, 1987.

Wright, John W. *The American Almanac of Jobs and Salaries*. 2d ed. New York: Avon, 1984.

Yoder, Janice. "Women at West Point: Lessons for Token Women in Male-Dominated Occupations." Pp. 523–37 in *Women: A Feminist Perspective*, ed. Jo Freeman. Mountain View, CA: Mayfield Publishing Co., 1989.

York, Reginald O., H. Carl Henley, and Dorothy N. Gamble. "Sexual Discrimination in Social Work: Is It Salary or Advancement?" *Social Work* 32 (1987): 336–40.

Young, Iris Marion. "Is Male Gender Identity the Cause of Male Domination?" Pp. 129–46 in *Mothering: Essays in Feminist Theory*, ed. Joyce Trebilcot. Totowa, NJ: Rowman and Allenheld, 1983.

Zimmer, Lynn. "Tokenism and Women in the Workplace." *Social Problems* 35 (1988): 64–77.

Index